BRINGING HOME
THE BACON

BRINGING HOME THE BACON

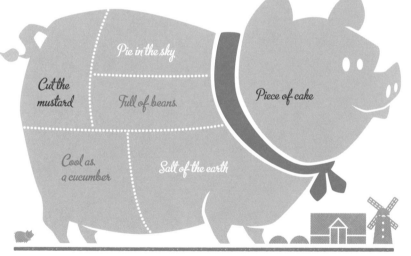

Pie in the sky

Cut the mustard

Full of beans

Piece of cake

Cool as a cucumber

Salt of the earth

CURIOUS CULINARY SAYINGS

THEIR ORIGINS & MEANINGS EXPLAINED

First published as Bringing Home the Bacon & Cutting the Mustard in 2000
Updated and reprinted for Lakeland in 2013

Packaged by Susanna Geoghegan Gift Publishing

Text © Susie Foster 2013

Cover design: Milestone Design
Typesetting: seagulls.net

Printed in China

INTRODUCTION

From the biblical story of Adam tasting the forbidden fruit in the Garden of Eden to Greek mythological tales involving troublemaking apples and the sweet-tasting fare of the gods, food and food-related sayings have long been influential ingredients in the development of language.

Indeed, if Britain's cuisine is sometimes accused of being insular and unimaginative, the same cannot be said of its mother tongue English, which has been nourished and enriched by other languages throughout its history. Words and expressions from the kitchen and dinner table, the farmyard and the market, have been introduced and adapted to English from other cultures and languages since the earliest times. References to 'salt' in the sense of 'wages', 'vintage' as a definition of special quality and 'larder' as a place to store provisions, for example, were all acquired from the Romans, and numerous expressions and turns of phrase to do with food and drink have migrated the short distance across the English Channel to England from France. Many French phrases, such as 'à la carte' and 'table d'hôte' have been imported directly into our everyday speech, while others have endured a more tortuous translation – 'bully beef', meaning salted or corned beef, and 'plonk', otherwise known as wine, were both derived from genuine French words, but in their somewhat enthusiastic adoption by British servicemen became the slang forms we use today.

The language of food reflects Britain's rich and chequered history, not just in the diversity of sources, which came with the expansion of the British Empire and the development of North America, but in the use to which that language has been put. The word 'cha' for 'tea' originated in China, 'barbecue' came out of the early language of Haiti, 'whisky', rather appropriately, was taken from Gaelic, and 'coffee' was acquired from Arabic, while Portuguese produced 'marmalade' and the language of the Aztecs gave us 'chocolate'.

At a basic level, the language of food can reveal something of medieval hospitality and the social hierarchy that was established in England after the

BRINGING HOME <u>THE</u> BACON

Norman Conquest in 1066, as demonstrated by expressions such as 'above the salt' and 'upper crust'. Phrases including 'bringing home the bacon', 'living high off the hog' and 'bacon brains' give an idea of the importance of livestock and meat, particularly the pig, as a main part of the early British diet. This is not a sterile process, however, frozen in some bygone era, for language is continually evolving, with new terms, such as 'beefcake' and 'couch potato', having only been coined and become commonplace within the last few decades.

The language of food has also been influenced by specific individuals and popular culture. Figures including the Australian operatic singer Dame Nellie Melba and John Montagu, 4th Earl of Sandwich, have guaranteed their place in history through the popularity of dishes such as peach Melba, Melba toast and of course the ubiquitous sandwich. Others, like Hiram Codd, who unwittingly led to the word 'codswallop', and Ben Wenberg, forever consigned to obscurity by the renaming of 'lobster Wenberg' to 'Newberg', made their contribution to the English language through less memorable means.

Over time, the meanings of many words have changed. 'Venison', for example, started out as a general term for any food gained in the course of a hunt; only later did it acquire the specific reference it has today. The same is true of 'claret'. The language of food also reflects the changing processes, techniques and fashions of cookery itself, as can be seen in phrases such as 'done to a turn' and 'the pot calling the kettle black', which hark back to the days when all cooking was done over an open fire, before the advent of the stove, which in turn gave rise to expressions such as 'on the back burner'. Then there are those quirks and anomalies which give language its spice and variety. In the case of food and drink, 'Welsh rarebit', 'Bombay duck' and even the seemingly obvious 'ploughman's lunch' make us pause and smile when we discover the stories behind their usage.

The English language offers a veritable feast of fascinating origins and histories waiting to be uncovered and enjoyed. Although only a selection of food sayings can be included here, it is hoped that this book will serve as an appetizing entrée into the subject, providing some interesting and intriguing food for thought.

Above the salt

In ancient times, salt was difficult to obtain, and yet highly prized, due to its ability to preserve food. Thus, strange as it may seem to us today, it was a rare and valuable commodity only available to the wealthy and the privileged. During the Middle Ages, the nobility would dine at the 'high table', and their servants and commoners would sit on surrounding lower tables. The salt cellar itself was seen as equally valuable and in prosperous households was given pride of place in the centre of the table. Only the most honoured members of the household and guests would be seated at the top end of the table, thus 'above the salt', while the more lowly diners sat further down, giving rise to the expression 'below the salt'. Both phrases have retained their social distinctions long after salt became the common household staple it now is, and long after such segregation at table ceased.

Adam's ale

A jocular term for water, 'Adam's ale' refers to the biblical story of Adam, who as the first man on earth drank the pure, clean waters of the Garden of Eden. Conversely, the 'demon drink', otherwise known as alcohol, was associated with the devil. The expression is still in common use, although in Scotland water is sometimes referred to as 'Adam's wine'.

ADAM'S
APPLE

☞ THE FAMILIAR NAME FOR THE PROTUBERANCE AT THE FRONT OF THE NECK, PARTICULARLY PROMINENT IN MEN, THE ADAM'S APPLE IS FORMED BY THE THYROID CARTILAGE AND TECHNICALLY KNOWN AS THE LARYNGEAL PROMINENCE. BEFORE THE ADVENT OF MODERN MEDICAL SCIENCE, HOWEVER, POPULAR FOLKLORE HELD THAT IT WAS FORMED WHEN A PIECE OF APPLE, COMMONLY THOUGHT TO BE THE FORBIDDEN FRUIT MENTIONED IN THE FIRST TESTAMENT, BECAME STUCK IN ADAM'S THROAT, ALTHOUGH THE BIBLE DOES NOT IN FACT STATE ANY PARTICULAR FRUIT.

After meat, mustard

This saying is used to refer to something which is either done, offered or arrives too late and so is no longer needed or of use, much like the phrase 'closing the door after the horse has bolted'. Of course, mustard has long been a favoured accompaniment to meat, but for most people would be wholly unappetizing if served on its own.

À la carte

Meaning 'according to the menu', this expression, like so many phrases in the language of wining and dining, is a French term – the word 'carte' translates literally as 'card', and refers to the menu. To dine à la carte therefore is to select a meal from a menu on which individual dishes are listed and priced separately, as opposed to table d'hôte, meaning 'host's table', which is a set menu offered at a fixed price.

All for heat and pilchards

A small fish related to the herring, the pilchard is commonly found around the coasts of Cornwall, where this expression was coined to describe warm, misty weather when it was likely that the sun would soon break out and that shoals of pilchards would be gathering ready for the fishermen.

All hands and the cook

Originating in the American West during the heyday of the cowboy in the second half of the nineteenth century, this unusual expression for a state of emergency referred to the necessity for everyone to help out on large cattle runs when the animals were restless and there was a risk of stampede. The inclusion of the cook, whose job was usually limited to supplying meals for the hungry cowboys, signified the urgency of the situation and the saying later came to be used more widely to imply a crisis of any kind.

All his geese are swans

A mature swan is a more attractive bird than a goose by most people's standards and this expression of self-delusion rests on just such a universal belief. Anyone who convinces himself that his children can do no wrong and that whatever he himself does is unmatchable in his own estimation can rightly be accused of believing that 'all his geese are swans'. The saying is also used in its reverse form, 'all his swans are geese', to imply that for all a person's fine promises and boastful expectations, these beliefs usually turn out to be ill-founded.

A lot on your plate

To have 'a lot on one's plate' means to feel overloaded with too much to deal with, the excess of food being a metaphor for life's commitments and duties. In polite society, having too much food piled high on your plate has long been regarded as a sign of greed, not to mention poor judgement, as recalled in the familiar reprimand of having 'eyes bigger than your stomach', used when food is left uneaten on the plate.

An apple a day keeps the doctor away

With the current health advice to eat at least five portions of fruit and vegetables a day, this well-known saying seems just as pertinent today as it did when a version first appeared in print as a 'Pembrokeshire proverb' in an edition of *Notes and Queries* magazine of 1866, which stated 'Eat an apple on going to bed, And you'll keep the doctor from earning his bread'. A similar expression is said to have originated in the West Country, as quoted in Elizabeth Mary Wright's *Rustic Speech and Folk-Lore* (1913): 'Ait a happle avore gwain to bed, An' you'll make the doctor bed his bread.'

Apple of discord

Meaning the cause or core of a dispute, this ancient phrase is derived from Greek mythology. Legend has it that the goddess Eris (Discord), furious at not being invited to the marriage of Thetis and Peleus, threw a golden apple inscribed with the words 'for the fairest' amidst the wedding guests during the festivities. This ignited an argument as to who was the most beautiful between the three goddesses Hera, Athena and Aphrodite, succeeding not only in disrupting the wedding, but eventually leading to the Trojan War.

Apple of his eye

This familiar phrase dates back to ancient biblical times, when it was used to refer to the actual pupil of the eye, most probably because in those days the pupil was believed to be a solid sphere, like an apple. It is mentioned several times in the Bible, notably '… he kept him as the apple of his eye' (Deuteronomy 32:10). Shakespeare used it too, in *A Midsummer Night's Dream*. The expression later came to be used figuratively to describe anything that is cherished or held particularly dear, as indeed sight is.

Apple-pie bed

An 'apple-pie' bed is a practical joke in which the bed is made with the sheets folded in such a way that it is impossible for anyone to actually get completely in. Despite the name, however, this mischief has little to do with either apples or pies. The most likely explanation is that the term may be derived from the French *nappe pliée*, meaning 'folded sheet' or 'folded linen'.

APPLE-PIE
ORDER

SOMETHING THAT IS NEAT AND PERFECTLY ARRANGED, WITH EVERYTHING IN ITS CORRECT PLACE, IS SAID TO BE IN 'APPLE-PIE ORDER'. ONCE AGAIN, THIS POPULAR TURN OF PHRASE IS MORE LIKELY TO HAVE BEEN BORROWED FROM FRENCH THAN BE RELATED TO ANYTHING CREATED IN A KITCHEN. THERE ARE TWO POSSIBLE CANDIDATES FOR ITS ORIGIN. THE FIRST, 'CAP-À- PIE', MEANING 'HEAD TO FOOT', DATES BACK TO THE OLD FRENCH OF THE MIDDLE AGES WHEN IT WAS USED TO REFER TO A KNIGHT WHO WAS READY FOR BATTLE AND FULLY ARMED FROM TOP TO TOE. THE SECOND POTENTIAL EXPLANATION AGAIN LIES IN THE EXPRESSION *NAPPE PLIÉE*, BUT WITH THE REFERENCE TO A FOLDED SHEET IN THIS INSTANCE BEING ONE OF THOROUGH, TIDY AND COMPLETE PREPARATION.

As a pig loves marjoram

For as long as pigs have been kept as domestic animals it has been known that they have a strong aversion to any of the aromatic plants belonging to the marjoram family. The now rarely heard expression 'as a pig loves marjoram' was first used by the Roman poet Lucretius as an emphatic form of 'not at all'.

As thin as Banbury cheese

Best known for its associations with Banbury Cross of nursery-rhyme fame, the market town of Banbury in Oxfordshire is also home to the less familiar Banbury cheese. No longer in commercial production, this rich, yellow cow's milk cheese was made in very thin rounds only an inch or so thick. To be regarded as 'as thin as Banbury cheese' therefore, is to be considered very thin indeed.

Attic salt

The term 'Attic' refers to the dialect spoken in ancient Athens. The Athenians were noted for their subtle, refined wit, which added a certain elegance to their literary works and conversation, in the way that a sprinkling of salt, then a highly esteemed commodity, could enhance the flavour of food. Over time, 'Attic salt' came to be applied to any example of wit displayed through a few classic, well-chosen words.

A watched pot never boils

These words of wisdom used as a mild reproof for impatience remind us that things only seem to take longer if you are watching and waiting for them to happen, although of course there is no literal truth in this idea. In the days when hungry families cooked all their meals in a single pot suspended over a fire, there must have been many a 'watched pot' and no doubt many a fraught cook!

Bacon brains

Bacon was once the only meat available to English peasants and therefore references to 'bacon' were generally disparaging. 'Bacon brains' is another way of calling someone a 'simpleton', or a 'slow-witted yokel'.

Baker's dozen

A 'baker's dozen' is made up of thirteen items as opposed to the traditional twelve. The practice of giving an extra loaf dates back to medieval times when bakers were subject to large fines if they sold bread that was underweight. To avoid this, they provided surplus loaves known as the 'in-bread'. The thirteenth loaf in a baker's dozen was called the 'vantage loaf'.

Banana republic

This derogatory term describes a small, often Third World, country or state with a fragile economy entirely dependent on the export of a single commodity controlled by a foreign capital. It was coined by the American writer O. Henry in his book *Cabbages and Kings* of 1904. The original 'banana republics' were the small Caribbean and Central American states that were funded in the early part of the twentieth century by big US corporations to develop the huge banana crop needed to supply the growing North American market. Once their prosperity and future growth were inextricably linked with growing and exporting bananas, they became known as 'banana republics'.

BARBECUE

WHEN CHRISTOPHER COLUMBUS LED HIS FIRST EXPEDITION TO THE CARIBBEAN IN 1492, HE AND HIS MEN ENCOUNTERED MANY NEW PRACTICES AND CUSTOMS, ONE OF WHICH WAS THE METHOD OF COOKING MEAT AND FISH ON A FRAMEWORK OF STICKS AND POSTS ABOVE A FIRE KNOWN LOCALLY AS *BARBACOA*, WHICH THAT FIRST SPANISH EXPEDITION BROUGHT BACK TO EUROPE WHEN THEY RETURNED. BY THE SEVENTEENTH CENTURY, 'BARBECUE' HAD ENTERED THE ENGLISH LANGUAGE AND IN DUE COURSE THE DEVICE ON WHICH FOOD COULD BE COOKED OUTDOORS WAS EXTENDED IN MEANING TO INCLUDE THE SOCIAL OCCASION AT WHICH SUCH FOOD WAS SERVED.

Barley sugar

Although traditionally made using barley, the popular old-fashioned boiled sweet 'barley sugar' probably acquired its unusual name from a mistranslation of the term *sucre brûlé*, which in French means 'burnt sugar'. In France, however, this term is no longer used, and the sweet is known by the name *sucre d'orge*, translating literally as 'sugar of barley'.

Barmecide Feast

A story in the *Arabian Nights* tells of a prince of the great Barmecide family who played an unkind trick on a starving pauper by the name of Schacabac. Inviting Schacabac to dine with him, the prince then presented his guest with a succession of empty plates, enquiring after each as to how Schacabac was enjoying his meal, to which the famished wretch replied politely in praise of the non-existent food. However, when offered imaginary wine, Schacabac saw his chance and, excusing himself by pretending to be drunk, knocked the prince down. Seeing the funny side of his reaction, Schacabac's host forgave him and served him with all the food and drink he could consume. From this story, a 'Barmecide Feast' has acquired the meaning of an illusion, notably one spiked with a great disappointment, i.e. something that promises much but delivers nothing.

Beanfeast

Originating in the early nineteenth century, a 'beanfeast' was traditionally an annual celebratory dinner given for employees by their employer, during which beans and bacon were always served. Today, a beanfeast can be used to describe any special outing or notable occasion, which may or may not involve a meal and almost certainly has very little to do with beans.

Beans are in flower

It was once believed that the scent of bean flowers made people light-headed. A person who was behaving in a foolish way would therefore be dismissed with the comment the 'beans are in flower'.

Beef

This is one of several common words connected with food that shed interesting light on the social order that was established in England following the Norman Conquest in the eleventh century. The Anglo-Saxon peasants working for their Norman overlords used various words for their animals, including the Middle English 'cou', which became cow. The French nobles, however, who only ever dined on the cooked meat, used the Old French word *boef*, meaning 'ox'. Hence two words evolved, one describing the actual animal and one the meat, as demonstrated in other English examples of animal- and food-related words such as pig and pork, and poultry and chicken.

Beefcake

Beef has long been associated with strength and vigour. Indeed, to put some 'beef' into something means to apply extra effort to it, hence the connection between 'beef' and muscularity. The term 'beefcake' has come to be used to refer to powerfully built male athletes and models, particularly in the media, and came about as a counterpart of the earlier pin-up pictures of young women, which were known as 'cheesecake'.

Beefeater

The Yeoman Warders of the Tower of London have long been known as 'Beefeaters', although the exact origins of the nickname are unknown. However, their position as part of the Royal Bodyguard since at least 1509 entitled them to eat meat from the King's table, and it therefore seems likely that this gave rise to the name. Indeed, in 1669 Count Cosimo, Grand Duke of Tuscany noted that the Yeomen Warders were given a 'very large ration of beef' on a daily basis. 'Eater' was once a synonym for a 'servant' and 'beefeaters' (servants who ate beef) were of higher rank than 'loaf-eaters', which was used to describe 'menial servants'. There is a suggestion that the name may have originated from the French *buffetier*, a term for servants who waited at the sideboard, but given the robust nature of a beefeater's role in guarding the Tower of London, consuming beef seems a more plausible explanation of the name than serving from a sideboard.

Beefing

This popular American term meaning to complain was probably coined from London's cockney rhyming slang, in which the cry of the honest citizen 'stop thief, stop thief' was mocked as 'hot beef, hot beef'. Thus to 'beef' came to mean 'make a fuss'.

Beer money

Between 1800 and 1823 British soldiers and NCOs received a daily allowance of one penny in lieu of an issue of beer. The practice has long been forgotten, but 'beer money' is still used to describe spare cash designated for spending on refreshments and treats.

Best thing since sliced bread

The automation of modern baking, which produces millions of identical loaves of sliced bread, was regarded as a major advance in food production by both producers and consumers. The first pre-sliced packaged loaves were marketed in the USA in 1928 as 'the greatest forward step in the baking industry since bread was wrapped', leading to the well-known phrase of universal approval, 'the best (or greatest) thing since sliced bread'.

Big Apple

'Big Apple' became a popular, and officially recognized, nickname for New York City following an advertising campaign to attract more visitors at the beginning of the 1970s. However, the term had already been in existence since at least the 1920s when it was used in reference to the city's many racecourses and popularized by the journalist John Fitzgerald working for the *New York Morning Telegraph*. By the end of the decade, the use of 'Big Apple' had spread to outside of the horseracing world and was particularly used by jazz musicians. In 1997, the corner of 54th and Broadway, where Fitzgerald lived, was renamed Big Apple Corner in his honour.

Big cheese

In days gone by, 'cheese' was used to describe something pleasant, of good quality, whereas today the term 'cheesy' has opposite connotations. The phrase 'big cheese', which seems to have come about in the USA in the early twentieth century and means an important or influential person, may have its roots in this earlier association, or may possibly be derived from the Persian and Urdu word *chiz*, meaning 'thing', thus the big 'thing'.

Boil down to

Since boiling reduces the volume of whatever is being boiled, this expression is a straightforward allusion to the cooking pot or kettle, in which something is reduced to its very essence, all extraneous material having been disposed of.

Bombay duck

'Bombay duck' is in fact not a bird of any kind; it is a fish, known as a 'bummalo', which, dried and salted, is eaten as a relish with curry. The bummalo is caught throughout South Asia, but its association with Bombay in this expression may stem from the Marathi name, *bombil*.

Boozing

'Boozing' is usually taken to be slang for drinking steadily and heavily, and is perhaps seen as a relatively modern expression. However, the history of the word shows that its pedigree reaches back to Middle English in which the verb *bousen* meant to 'drink deeply'. This was probably associated with the Dutch *buizen* and the German *bousen*, both meaning 'to drink to excess'.

Born with a silver spoon in your mouth

This much-used phrase alludes to the children of well-to-do parents. Silver spoons used to be common christening presents, but a wealthy child had no need to wait until their christening to get one – they could have silver spoons, and all the wealth that their use implied, from the moment they were born.

Bottle up

To 'bottle up' one's feelings means to contain them and hold them in control, an allusion to the process of bottling preserves and drinks, which enables them to be set aside secure and undisturbed for use at a later date. But while bottling food and drink may be sensible, emotional bottling up may not always be a good thing – once the 'bottle' has been opened the contents are released, and the result can be an emotional outburst from someone who has been keeping themselves in check for some time.

Bread and butter

The phrase 'bread and butter' is commonly used to refer to someone's livelihood or main source of basic income, with no extras or additional benefits. A 'bread and butter letter', however, means a short thank-you note to someone who has provided hospitality.

Breadwinner

'Bread', according to the old proverb, 'is the staff of life' and indeed bread, in one form or another, is a staple food the world over. A 'breadwinner' is the person who provides that staple commodity. The word has therefore come to be generally applied to the member of a family who is responsible for supporting the family financially.

Bringing home the bacon

It has been suggested that the origins of this familiar saying date back to a ritual known as the Dunmow Flitch trials, which began in the early twelfth century when a church in Great Dunmow, Essex, challenged married couples to swear marital devotion in front of the congregation, with the most convincing taking home a 'flitch' (side) of bacon. This tradition has continued to be held in the village every four years (see also 'Eating Dunmow bacon'). Because pigs represented the only meat that many families ever ate, for hundreds of years a pig was also the sought-after prize at country fairs. Bowling for a pig, for example, was a popular rural pastime enjoyed on feast days and other holidays, as was catching a greased pig. In both cases the winner was rewarded with a pig to take home and 'bringing home the bacon' became a popular term for winning a prize, or succeeding in some form of contest, and eventually came to mean to earn money, particularly for the family, or to be financially successful.

Broaching your claret

In the boxing ring 'claret' was adopted as a word for 'blood' because of its dark red colour. In order to draw claret (or any other liquid) from a barrel, the barrel has to be 'broached' with a tap. So in boxing 'broaching your claret' came to mean 'giving you a bloody nose'.

BROWSE
HIS JIB

ABOARD A SAILING SHIP, 'BROWSING THE JIB' MEANT HAULING THE TRIANGULAR SAIL THAT IS SET FORWARD OF THE MAST – THE JIB SAIL – TAUT; IN OTHER WORDS MAKING IT TIGHT. BY ASSOCIATION, A SAILOR WHO MADE HIMSELF 'TIGHT' THROUGH OVER-INDULGENCE WAS SAID TO HAVE 'BROWSED HIS JIB'. 'JIB' HERE REFERS TO HIS FACE AND 'BROWSE' MEANS TO FATTEN; AN APT DESCRIPTION OF WHAT HAPPENS WHEN THE CONSUMPTION OF TOO MUCH ALCOHOL RESULTS IN A FLUSHED AND PUFFY FACE.

Bubble and squeak

Originally made from meat and potatoes, 'bubble and squeak' is now a term that refers to a snack made by frying potatoes with other leftover vegetables, usually cabbage, from a roast dinner. The origins of the term are unknown, but it's likely that 'bubble and squeak' is so-named because of the noise the ingredients make when cooked – while being boiled the potatoes and greens 'bubble' and, once transferred to the frying pan, they 'squeak' in the hot oil.

Bully beef

'Bully beef' originated in the armed services where it became a principal component of naval and military rations towards the end of the nineteenth century, and continued to be issued as standard rations well into the twentieth. In the army 'bully beef' referred to tinned, salted beef (or corned beef); in the Royal Navy it was the name given to boiled salt beef. Both are derived from the French for 'boiled beef' – *boeuf bouilli*, from the verb *bouillir* meaning 'to boil' – and *bouilli* was printed on the labels of tinned rations of beef supplied during the Franco-Prussian war of 1870–71.

Bunting

Any connection between the decorative strings of flags hung up for high days and holidays and the language of food may not be immediately apparent, but originally bunting was not made from the pretty, light fabrics that we are familiar with today. Instead, it was traditionally made from a strong, gauzy woollen cloth that was spun for sifting flour. In the West Country such sifting was known as 'bunting' and it seems likely that the material acquired this name – and subsequently the decorative flags too, when the fabric was re-used in this way for special occasions.

Butter

The obvious effects of spreading butter on a piece of plain bread are to both enhance its flavour and coat it with a smooth surface, leading to the figurative use of 'butter' in phrases such as 'to butter up', meaning to 'flatter' and 'smooth' someone down in order to get them to do what you want. The allusion to the smoothness and greasiness of butter extends to the sporting field as well, where 'butterfingers' is a term of exasperation levelled at anyone who drops an easy catch, a phrase which has also 'spread' to be used in everyday situations of clumsiness.

Butter wouldn't melt in his mouth

One of the gastronomic delights of butter is its melting point, which is close enough to body temperature that it melts when eaten. The phrase 'butter wouldn't melt in his mouth', however, suggests that a person has such a cool demeanour, and is so prim and proper, that this simply wouldn't happen. Often used in a mildly critical manner, to suggest that someone is guilty of something although they may look innocent, the phrase is frequently used in the shorter, simpler form 'butter wouldn't melt'.

Buttering your bread on both sides

Both in action and meaning, 'buttering your bread on both sides' indicates both wasteful extravagance and luxury, and also equates to the similar turn of phrase 'having the best of both worlds'. An individual 'buttering his bread on both sides' is seeking or achieving advantage from two sides at the same time, or simply doing two things simultaneously and benefiting from them both.

Cabbage

Although the spelling is the same as that of the familiar green vegetable with a round heart, in the tailor's workshop 'cabbage' developed an entirely independent meaning to that in the greengrocer's shop or market garden. From the seventeenth century, 'cabbage' was the term applied to pieces of cloth cut off by tailors and kept as a perk of the trade. As a result, tailors were sometimes nicknamed 'cabbages'. Outside the tailoring profession 'cabbage' acquired the broader meaning of 'pilfer', which links it with the Old French *cabas* meaning 'deceit' and 'theft', and the Dutch *kabassen*, 'to pilfer'.

Café au lait spots

Café au lait is made by mixing equal quantities of coffee and hot milk. The resulting drink is therefore light brown in colour and this has led to the use of 'café au lait' to describe anything that is a similar shade of brown. By extension, the term 'café au lait spots' is sometimes used to refer to light-brown freckles on the surface of the skin.

Cafeteria

The first 'cafeteria' opened for business on 4 September 1885 on New Street in New York City. Called the Exchange Buffet, this was a self-service restaurant, which led the way in a developing global market for what were to become 'fast-food' restaurants of every description. The name is derived from *cafeteria*, a Mexican-Spanish term for 'coffee shop'.

Cakes and ale

Like 'beer and skittles', 'cakes and ale' epitomizes the simple pleasures of life and has come to mean a good time in general. The expression appeared as the title of a novel by well-known British writer Somerset Maugham in 1930.

Cat-lap

Towards the end of the eighteenth century, 'cat-lap' was used to refer to any thin beverage, notably milk or weak tea, implying that it was only fit for the cat. The same associations are found in 'cat-nap', a brief snooze whilst sitting, which originated in the middle of the nineteenth century.

Cellar

Nowadays, the word 'cellar' when used on its own is generally taken to mean a wine cellar. However, from the thirteenth century 'cellar' was applied to a storeroom housing a range of commodities; it was only a century later that it acquired the further definition as an underground storeroom. 'Cellar' in this sense is an English adaptation of the Old French *celier*, which was itself derived from the Latin for a storeroom, *cella*. The other English use of the word 'salt cellar' is a corruption of the French *salièr* meaning 'salt dish'.

Cheesecake

The female counterpart of 'beefcake', the slang term 'cheesecake' dates from the 1930s and was used to refer to pin-up photographs of glamorous young women in the media. Why 'cheesecake' should have been chosen as an appropriate description remains unclear, although it may be a reference to the earlier American phrase 'better than cheesecake', presumably meant as the ultimate compliment when comparing someone or something to this luxury dessert.

Cheesed off

'Cheesed off', like 'browned off' has meant 'fed up' or 'disgruntled' since the middle of the nineteenth century – there is a reference to 'cheese' in a similar context in Charles Dickens's novel *The Old Curiosity Shop* (1841). The exact origins of the phrase are uncertain, but when a cheese goes off it turns sour and loses its appeal, and when overheated it spoils and turns brown, so it could be said that 'cheesed off ' and 'browned off' are closely related in both the culinary and figurative senses.

Cherry picking

Since cherries have traditionally been picked by hand, there has always been an element of selection in choosing the ripest and most succulent fruit. From the country orchard, the expression has passed into modern corporate life, where 'cherry picking' has become widely used. to imply choosing the best and disregarding anything below a certain standard. Following the acquisition of one business interest by another, for example, the dominant partner may be accused of 'cherry picking' if it selects the most profitable areas of the business and concentrates on maximizing returns from them at the expense of others which perform less well.

CHESTNUT

WHEN USED TO REFER TO A TIRED OLD JOKE THAT MOST LISTENERS HAVE HEARD MANY TIMES BEFORE, THE TERM 'CHESTNUT' RECALLS A LONG-FORGOTTEN NINETEENTH-CENTURY MELODRAMA, *THE BROKEN SWORD*, IN WHICH ONE OF THE CHARACTERS REPEATS THE SAME JOKES, WITH JUST A FEW SMALL CHANGES. DURING ONE PARTICULAR SCENE, A JOKE INVOLVING A CORK TREE IS TOLD, WHICH CAUSES ANOTHER CHARACTER TO INTERRUPT SAYING THAT THE TREE WAS ACTUALLY A CHESTNUT. TO EMPHASIZE THE POINT, HE CONTINUES THAT HE HAS HEARD THE SAME JOKE TWENTY-SEVEN TIMES AND IS ABSOLUTELY SURE BY NOW THAT THE TREE IS A CHESTNUT. THE EXPRESSION WAS POPULARIZED IN THEATRICAL CIRCLES ON BOTH SIDES OF THE ATLANTIC BEFORE IT PASSED INTO GENERAL USE.

Chocolate

It is easy to forget that when chocolate first came to Europe from Central America in the sixteenth century it was served as a drink rather than the solid form of confectionery that is now so ubiquitous. It was Spanish explorers who first came across chocolate when they encountered the Aztec civilization in present-day Mexico. The Aztecs used cacao seeds to produce a type of food they called *chocolatl* and a similar sounding word *cacaua-atl* was a drink made from cacao. The invaders from Europe blended the two to produce *chocolate*, and this term was adopted to refer to the produce of the cacao berry in both its solid and liquid state.

Chocolate-box

The first eating chocolate to be produced on a factory scale had been manufactured in Vevey, Switzerland, in 1819, by François-Louis Cailler, but the first British chocolate bar only appeared in 1847 and was made by J.S. Fry & Sons, followed by the Cadbury Brothers in 1849. It was not until 1875 that the first milk chocolate was manufactured, once again in Vevey. By the late nineteenth century, however, the chocolate confectionary business was well established, helped no doubt by the sentimental pictures which were chosen to decorate many chocolate-boxes. In 1868, Fry's chocolate assortment was packed in a box decorated with a picture of children in a goat carriage, and in the same year Richard Cadbury produced a portrait of his six-year-old daughter as the first commercial design of what was to become known as 'chocolate-box art', thus setting a pattern for the ornate or overtly sentimental designs that came to epitomize 'chocolate-box' style and decoration. The expression is often used, too, to describe places or buildings, or photographs of them – particularly in rural areas – that are especially pretty.

Chowder

'Chowder', a stew or thick soup usually made from fish, notably clams, heralds from the eastern seaboard of North America and probably owes its origins to the fishermen from Brittany who settled in the area in order to fish the Grand Banks, the famous fishing grounds which lie south-east of Newfoundland. Originally, it would have been a staple, basic food, but numerous variants have been created over the years, and in all parts of the world, including rich, creamy chowders served in high-class restaurants. The word 'chowder' itself probably came from the French *chaudière*, meaning a cooking pot, as featured in the phrase *faire la chaudière*, which was commonly used in Breton fishing villages to refer to the preparation of a pot with savoury condiments in which a fish stew could then be cooked.

Claret

Used to refer to red wines, and in recent times to the wines of Bordeaux specifically, the English term 'claret' was originally used to distinguish yellowish or light red wines from white wines. Today *clairet* in French refers to any local light-red wine and in Old French *vin claret* was similarly applied to pale-coloured wines as distinct from white wines – the word *vin* ('wine') was dropped from the English language when speaking of non-white wines.

Close as a Kentish oyster

For centuries, Kent has been renowned for the quality of its oysters. Since all oysters need to be tightly closed to ensure that they are good to eat, oysters from Kent were regarded as being particularly good because they were shut tighter than most. Thus anything described as being 'close as a Kentish oyster' was similarly shut fast. In time, this developed into the term's wider meaning of 'absolutely secret'.

Cobbler

In the language of food and drink, 'cobbler' is a word that may refer to both a pie and a mixed drink. The origins of both are obscure. 'Cobbler' the drink is a blend of wine (usually sherry), sugar, lemon and crushed ice, which is taken through a straw. Its name may come from a slang use of 'cobble' meaning 'to patch up', in the sense that those who drank it finished 'patched up', in other words well and truly drunk. Another suggestion is that 'cobbler' is an abbreviation for 'cobbler's punch': this was an unappealing-sounding drink made from gin and water, to which treacle and vinegar were added. When it comes to 'cobbler' the pie, its origin may be easier to pinpoint. This deep fruit or meat pie is topped with a crust made from a dough similar to scones or plain cakes, which is formed into balls or circles and laid over the topping. This gives it the appearance of cobblestones, from which the name 'cobbler' may have arisen.

Cocktail

The first recorded use of 'cocktail' appeared in a 1798 edition of London's *Morning Post*, but the first definition of the word can be traced to the American periodical *The Balance* in 1806, which described the drink as 'a stimulating liquor, composed of spirits of any kind, sugar, water, and bitters – it is vulgarly called *bittered sling* and is supposed to be an excellent electioneering potion'. Whether that 'potion' met with any success is not recorded, but it is known that by that time *coquetel* was a popular mixed drink in the Gironde district of south-west France. Given the similarity of name and contents, this seems as plausible an explanation of the origin of the term, 'cocktail' as any other, although these days of course a cocktail may comprise all manner of alcoholic or non-alcoholic ingredients. The word has also come to be applied to food as well as drink, and describes dishes which comprise a mixture of ingredients, such as a seafood cocktail.

Codswallop

To describe an idea or suggestion as 'codswallop' is summarily to dismiss it as utter nonsense, especially when it is offered as serious information or instruction. The term was possibly derived from the name of the English soft drinks maker Hiram Codd, who, in 1875, invented a new kind of mineral-water bottle using a glass marble as a stopper – when the bottle was shaken, the pressure forced the marble against the neck. Given that beer was colloquially known as 'wallop', it is likely that 'codd' was added to this as a disparaging term amongst drinkers for all non-alcoholic drinks. As the expression became more widely used, the spelling changed to 'codswallop' and the meaning was broadened to include anything dismissed as 'rubbish'.

Coffee

'Coffee' first arrived in Europe from southern Arabia via Turkey, so it is natural that its name in various European languages should reflect its point of origin. In fact 'coffee', *café* in French and *caffè* in Italian, comes from the Turkish *kahveh*, which in turn came from the Arabic for 'coffee', *qahwah*.

Cold fish

Anyone lacking in warm feelings or appearing unemotional and impassive could be described as a 'cold fish', following the widely held conviction that all fish are cold-blooded and therefore incapable of feeling.

Colonial goose

This Australian dish was developed on sheep stations to vary the unrelenting diet of plain mutton. In reality it has nothing to do with a goose. Instead it comprises a boned leg of mutton stuffed with breadcrumbs, herbs and onion before being roasted.

Condiments

'Condiments' used to season and flavour food have been known in English since the fifteenth century. The English word comes directly from Latin, in which *condimentum* carries the same meaning.

Cooking the books

Falsifying accounts is colloquially referred to as 'cooking the books', perhaps because changing the figures to create a set of results that suits your particular purpose is similar to the art of taking basics foodstuffs and transforming them into something different and more appealing by means of 'cooking'.

Cooking your goose

The first time this expression, which means to bring about the ruin or downfall of another – or oneself, in the case of cooking one's own goose – appeared in print was in around 1850. It is thought to have been a line in a popular play in which one of the characters decides that to 'save his own bacon' he must, in turn, 'cook another's goose'. There is no reliable evidence to explain why the goose is the chosen bird, or indeed why cooking it should be so significant. It may possibly refer to a goose being fattened for the table where it is due to take pride of place on a special occasion, but which is eaten prematurely leaving nothing for the actual event for which it has been designated.

Cool as a cucumber

Since ancient times, cucumbers have been known to maintain a cool temperature and it may therefore be no accident that they were first extensively propagated in the hot climates of India and the Near East. This characteristic has led to the popular simile 'as cool as a cucumber' when referring to someone who remains perfectly composed in all circumstances.

COUCH
POTATO

TEMPTING AS IT IS TO SEE THE SHAPE OF THE POTATO AS A KEY ELEMENT IN THIS POPULAR TURN OF PHRASE, ITS HISTORY SUGGESTS THAT THIS MAY BE COINCIDENTAL – ALTHOUGH IN SOME CASES 'COUCH POTATOES' MAY WELL BE POTATO-SHAPED, THIS DOES NOT APPEAR TO BE A PREREQUISITE IN QUALIFYING FOR THE CLASSIFICATION. THE NAME 'COUCH POTATO' FIRST CAME ABOUT IN AMERICA IN THE LATE 1970S, IN RECOGNITION OF THOSE WHO SPEND TOO LONG SLUMPED IN FRONT OF A TELEVISION RATHER THAN TAKING PART IN OTHER FORMS OF ENTERTAINMENT OR EXERCISE. IN AMERICA 'BOOB TUBE' IS SLANG FOR A TELEVISION SET AND IT MAY BE THE PUN ON 'TUBE/TUBER' THAT WAS RESPONSIBLE FOR THE POTATO ASSOCIATION IN THE PHRASE.

Crackers

The literal meaning of 'crackers' – crisp, savoury biscuits – bears little relation to it figurative use, which is an abbreviation for the expression 'crack-brained'. The meaning, as the wording suggests, is 'slightly mad' or 'eccentric'.

Cry barley

'Barley' in this usage is a variant of 'parley', the cry for truce in rough-and-tumble games enjoyed for hundreds of years. 'Cry Barley' was itself the name of a country game, similar to 'Prisoner's Base', in which players made use of a 'home' called 'hell'.

Cup of cha

'Cha' is the Anglicized form of the Mandarin Chinese word for tea. Its use in English is first recorded in the early seventeenth century and since then 'cup of cha' has become widely used as an alternative to 'cup of tea'. A similar word occurs in several Indian languages and the adoption of these during the British rule of India helped to popularize the expression.

Curate's egg

A cartoon in *Punch* magazine dating from 1895 gave rise to the expression 'good in parts, like the curate's egg'. In the cartoon, a nervous young curate is seated at his bishop's breakfast table, when the bishop announces, 'I'm afraid you've got a bad egg, Mr Jones!' The curate, desperate not to offend, replies, 'Oh no, my Lord, I assure you! Parts of it are excellent!' From this, the expression 'good in parts, like the curate's egg' took hold, and has come to describe something 'patchy' and of 'uneven quality'.

Cut the mustard

When someone is said to have 'cut the mustard' it means that they have done a thing well, particularly when it was suspected beforehand that they might not. As well as being a popular condiment, 'mustard' became a slang term for 'the best'. The origins of this saying are unclear. One school of thought favours the idea that the 'cutting' relates to the harvesting of a notoriously difficult plant to glean, thereby implying that only the best can undertake the task. Another suggests that the term comes from the practice of adding vinegar to 'cut' or reduce the bitterness of the mustard seeds when creating the familiar paste (the simile 'as keen as mustard' alludes to the sharpness of the condiment), while yet another puts forward the notion that the term is a confusion of the military expression 'cut the muster', which means well turned out both in appearance and punctuality. Whatever its origin, it is patently clear that *not* to 'cut the mustard' signifies a failure to achieve the required standard.

Different as chalk and cheese

Chalk and cheese share a superficial similarity of appearance, in that chalk and a good many cheeses are white and fine-grained. Beyond that the two are poles apart. So the phrase 'different as chalk and cheese' is an emphatic statement of difference.

Dine with Duke Humphrey

Far from being entertained to a lavish meal, to 'dine with Duke Humphrey' has historically meant going without dinner altogether. Humphrey, the Duke of Gloucester, was the youngest son of Henry IV and renowned for his generosity and hospitality. When he died it was rumoured that a monument would be erected to him in St Paul's Cathedral. In reality it never was, but another tomb was popularly supposed to be his and people seeking sanctuary within the church's precinct, and consequently with no dinner to go to, would say they were to 'dine with Duke Humphrey' that night. The expression was well understood in its day, as was a similar but later one, to 'sup with Sir Thomas Gresham'. Gresham was the merchant financier who founded and built the Royal Exchange, which, business apart, became a favourite haunt for loungers. Both expressions remained in common use until the early nineteenth century.

Dining with the cross-legged knights

To 'dine with the cross-legged knights' is to go without any dinner at all. The 'crossed-legged knights' referred to were the stone effigies of Templar knights in their old Temple Church in London, which later became a meeting place for lawyers and their clients. This was also the haunt of layabouts who frequented the Temple on the off-chance of being hired as witnesses.

Dish up spurs

During the Middle Ages, the border separating England from Scotland was the scene of local vendettas and guerrilla campaigns. Scottish raiders invariably returned home with rustled English cattle, on which the chieftain's household fed. When supplies of beef began to run low, the lady of the household would send up a pair of spurs as the last course to show her menfolk that it was time to don their spurs and carry out another raid south of the border to replenish the laird's larder.

Doing porridge

Slang for 'spending time in prison', this phrase increased in popularity with the success of the 1970s sitcom *Porridge*. Its origin is said to be from the rhyming slang 'borage and thyme', meaning 'time' behind bars, but it may also refer to the fact that porridge was once a staple food in prison.

Done to a turn

This phrase, still used in modern cookery, dates back to the medieval kitchen, where joints and other meats were cooked on a spit above the fire. To ensure that everything was cooked evenly, the spit was slowly rotated, exposing each face of the meat to an equal amount of heat. Meat that was 'done to a turn' was cooked exactly right; one more turn on the spit would have overcooked it. Away from the kitchen, 'done to a turn' refers to other activities that are satisfactorily completed.

Don't count your chickens before they are hatched

This long-established saying warns not to make, or act on, an assumption, which may turn out to be wrong even if the prospects appear to be favourable. The proverb is based on Aesop's fable about a milkmaid, who, so preoccupied with the eggs she was going to buy with the proceeds from her milk, lost concentration and spilt the milk that would have provided the wherewithal for the eggs.

Don't put all your eggs in one basket

This well-known caution first appeared in print in an Italian book of proverbs in 1662, although it had probably been in use before then, and carries a clear warning – it is better to spread the risk than chance everything on a single venture.

Doughboy

The precise origins of this informal reference to American infantrymen are not clear, but it first appeared during the Mexican-American War of 1846–8. Some sources suggest that the term may have arisen from the soldier's uniforms, which were fastened with distinctive large brass buttons resembling the so-called 'doughboy' dumplings usually eaten by sailors and soldiers, while others cite the Mexican terrain itself as the reason for the nickname – the dry, parched soil was said to leave a coating of dust over the soldiers, rather like flour, hence 'doughboy'.

Drinking at Freeman's Quay

Anyone said to be 'drinking at Freeman's Quay' is enjoying a drink at someone else's expense. It is said that porters and carmen could once receive a free pot of beer at Freeman's Quay near London Bridge, which may have given rise to the expression. However, it seems more likely that the word 'Freeman' itself gives us the clue as to this saying's origins.

DRINKING A
TOAST

IN ELIZABETHAN TIMES, IT WAS CUSTOMARY TO ADD A PIECE OF SPICED TOAST TO CUPS OF WINE AND ALE TO ENHANCE THEIR FLAVOUR. STRANGE AS THIS MAY APPEAR, IT IS PERHAPS NO MORE BIZARRE THAN THE STORY IN A VERY EARLY EDITION OF *TATLER* MAGAZINE, WHICH INTRODUCED THE PRACTICE OF DRINKING 'TOASTS' AS A GESTURE OF GOODWILL TO INDIVIDUALS OR INSTITUTIONS. ACCORDING TO THIS ACCOUNT, DURING THE REIGN OF CHARLES II A RENOWNED BEAUTY WAS IN THE CROSS BATH AT BATH WHEN ONE OF HER ADMIRERS TOOK A GLASS OF THE WATER IN WHICH SHE WAS STANDING AND DRANK HER HEALTH TO ALL PRESENT. THIS PROMPTED ANOTHER GENTLEMAN, WHO HAD BEEN INDULGING IN A RATHER STRONGER DRINK THAN WATER, TO EXCLAIM THAT HE WOULD JUMP IN THE WATER, FOR, 'THOUGH HE LIKED NOT THE LIQUOR, HE WOULD HAVE THE TOAST', IN OTHER WORDS THE LADY HERSELF. THEREAFTER, COMPLIMENTS EXPRESSED PUBLICLY AND ACCOMPANIED BY A DRINK BECAME KNOWN AS 'TOASTS'.

Drop like a hot potato

Most of us are all too aware of how hot a potato can become when baked in an oven at high temperature, particularly when eagerly removed with bare hands. By analogy, a 'hot potato' has come to mean a situation or predicament that is 'too hot to handle', one that may bring harm to you in some way. So to drop something 'like a hot potato' means to get rid of it very quickly, before it harms you or your interests.

Drowning the miller

Even millers, whose livelihoods depend on a constant flow of water to turn the waterwheels of their mills, would be overwhelmed by the volume of water alluded to in 'drowning the miller'. The hyperbole is an amusing criticism applied to an excessive amount of water added to spirits or tea. The implication is that the water dilutes them to the point of being almost tasteless and scarcely worth drinking.

Drunk as blazes

In this expression, 'blazes' refers not simply to fire, but to the devil or hell – therefore to be 'drunk as blazes' is to be very drunk indeed. Another possible explanation is that the term may derive from a corruption of 'blaiziers' or 'Blaisers', referring to guild members who enthusiastically threw themselves into the drinking and revelry that honoured the martyr St Blaise, the patron saint of woolcombers, on his feast day.

Earn your salt

In ancient Rome, soldiers were paid an allowance to buy salt, which was known as *salarium* (*sal* meaning 'salt' in Latin), giving rise to the word 'salary'. To 'earn your salt' is therefore to earn a salary.

Easy as pie

The reference here is more than likely to eating a pie rather than making one, since 'easy as pie' refers to anything that is ridiculously simple.

Eating Dunmow bacon

'Eating Dunmow bacon' is a well-established term to describe a happily married life and dates back to Dunmow in Essex in the early twelfth century, when tradition held that any person who could honestly swear, and prove, that for the previous twelve months and a day he or she had neither had a row with their spouse nor wished themselves unmarried, could claim a gammon of bacon, known as a 'flitch'.

Eating the leek

In William Shakespeare's play *Henry V*, written around 1599, the Welsh captain Fluellen is affronted by soldier Pistol's insults directed at the leek he proudly wears in his cap to the point where his anger boils over and he beats Pistol until he eats the leek, leaves and all. In allusion to this, 'to eat the leek' means being forced 'to eat your words', or 'take back' something you have said.

EGGHEAD

SLANG FOR 'HIGHBROW' OR 'INTELLECTUAL', AN 'EGGHEAD' IS ALSO BY ASSOCIATION SOMEONE WHO IS BALD; BALDNESS AND INTELLECTUAL QUALITIES GOING HAND IN HAND IN THIS CONTEXT. SINCE BALDNESS RESULTS IN A SMOOTH DOMED SCALP SIMILAR TO AN EGGSHELL, A BALD PERSON BECAME KNOWN AS AN 'EGGHEAD'.

Egg on

The 'egg' referred to here is an Old Norse word for the sharp side of a blade. This makes the sense of 'egg on', meaning to 'urge' and 'encourage', easier to understand. Anyone 'encouraged' by the cutting edge of a sword or dagger is more than likely to comply with what is requested. Used in this context, 'egg' is thought to be related to the Latin *acies*, meaning 'sharpness' as well as 'the edge of a blade'; *acus*, a 'thorn' or 'needle' in Latin, has a similar origin.

Eggs is eggs

Here is another instance of a word being misapplied in a commonly used expression – in this case, the 'eggs' in question owe more to mathematics than to hens. The phrase 'as sure as eggs is eggs' means 'completely safe' and 'absolutely certain'. Both carry the sense of irrefutable logic, which is regularly found in mathematics, leading to the general assumption that the expression originated in the mathematical statement 'as sure as x is x'.

Egg-trot

To ride to market with a load of eggs carried in panniers would have required a steady gait to avoid breaking the shells. The term 'egg-trot' therefore came about to mean a cautious jog-trot pace that avoids any undue shocks or exertion.

Every bean has its black

An old Roman saying, 'every bean has its black' refers to the black 'eye' found in many beans and carries the meaning that 'each of us has our own faults'.

Fiasco

Today a 'fiasco' is such a familiar expression for a failure or breakdown in general that its earlier connection with a dramatic or musical performance is frequently overlooked. However, the origin of that association is even more obscure, stemming as it does from the word *fiasco*, Italian for 'bottle' or 'flask'. In Italian theatre, the term *far fiasco*, meaning 'make a bottle', traditionally describes a failed performance and it is in this sense that the word entered the English language in the nineteenth century.

Fine kettle of fish

A 'fine kettle of fish' – sometimes a 'pretty kettle of fish' – means a 'muddle', or a 'messy business', and refers to the riverside picnic of the same name that forms a part of the traditional salmon fishing season in parts of Scotland. In this 'kettle of fish', freshly caught salmon are immediately put into a pot of boiling water right on the river bank. As soon as the fish are cooked, they are eaten by hand. Delicious as the result may be, the process is understandably messy, which accounts for its association with an unfortunate predicament.

Fine words butter no parsnips

At one time parsnips were more widely eaten than they are today and by tradition they were served with butter to enhance their flavour. 'Fine words butter no parsnips' is an old saying recorded from the early seventeenth century and appears in various versions, all with the same meaning: that words alone will not feed a family.

FISH
OUT OF
WATER

TO BEHAVE LIKE A 'FISH OUT OF WATER' IS TO APPEAR ILL AT EASE AWAY FROM YOUR FAMILIAR ENVIRONMENT. THIS AGE-OLD ALLUSION TO A FISH FLOUNDERING ON LAND OR THE DECK OF A FISHING BOAT IS AS RELEVANT TODAY AS IT ALWAYS HAS BEEN.

Fishwife

In days gone by it was common for a fisherman's wife to take her husband's most recent catch to market. There she did her utmost to make sure that everything was sold before any of the fish started to turn bad, which required her to hawk her wares loudly and with increasing vehemence as the day wore on. Despite the fact that this was necessary to her livelihood, the term 'fishwife' subsequently came to be applied to any loud, coarse-mannered woman, particularly one prone to shouting or yelling where others could hear her.

Flapjack

Flat batter cakes, baked on a griddle or in a shallow pan, were called 'flapjacks' because, like pancakes, they were once turned by being tossed in the air. In the course of this action, their shape seems to have been likened to the flapping of a bird's wing. In some countries, 'flapjack' is still used to describe a type of pancake, although in the UK, a flapjack is a quite different confection made of oats and syrup, and cooked in an oven.

Flat as a pancake

When poured into the frying pan, pancake batter usually spreads out to cover the surface of the pan in a thin, even layer, giving rise to the expression as 'flat as a pancake', meaning very flat indeed.

Flavour of the month

Competition in the ice cream business in America during the 1930s led to ice cream parlours across the country promoting their business by featuring a special 'flavour of the month', often at a reduced price to attract custom. By the 1980s the phrase had come to describe anything or anyone temporarily in vogue.

Forbidden fruit

The earliest reference to the 'forbidden fruit' appears in the second chapter of the Book of Genesis, when God warns Adam, the first man, 'Of every tree of the garden thou mayest freely eat: But of the tree of the knowledge of good and evil, thou shalt not eat of it: for in the day that thou eatest thereof thou shalt surely die.' From this, 'forbidden fruit' has come to mean 'forbidden' or 'unlawful pleasure' of any kind, particularly illicit love.

Forking out

From the late seventeenth century, the 'forks' was a slang term for the forefinger and middle finger, probably because together they resembled a two-pronged, V-shaped fork. In the criminal underworld, to 'fork' was to pickpocket, digging into other people's pockets and purses, and from this usage came the expression 'forking out', meaning 'handing over' or 'paying up'.

Four-ale bar

This phrase does not, as it might first appear, refer to the number of beverages available at an establishment. Instead, it is a reference to the price of the drink on offer, and a 'four-ale bar' would be a popular choice for those with little money to spare. At one time, the cheapest beer was sold at a cost of fourpence a quart, which equated to twopence a pint (less than a penny a pint in modern currency), thus public bars selling this cheap ale became known as 'four-ale bars'.

French cream

'French cream' became an alternative word for brandy following the French custom of adding a glass of brandy to an after-dinner cup of coffee in place of the more usual cream.

Fritter away

Although the spelling of 'fritter' is identical in both its common uses, the two words have no other association. The 'fritter' that is something coated in batter and fried in hot oil is ultimately derived from the Latin *frigere*, meaning 'to fry'. However, when the same spelling is applied to 'fritter away', in the sense of 'waste' and 'squander', its origin is related to the eighteenth-century term 'fritters', meaning 'fragments', which itself derived from the earlier word 'fitters' or pieces.

Fudge

'Fudge', like 'fritter' above, occurs in English with two distinct meanings. The most recent, dating from the second half of the nineteenth century, is the familiar confectionery made from butter, sugar and milk or cream. When 'fudge' is used as a verb, however, as in 'fudging' an issue, the meaning and origin is much older – by the seventeenth century 'fudge' had come to be used in the sense of 'patching up' and 'faking', which stemmed from the Middle English *fage*, meaning to 'deceive' and 'beguile'.

Full of beans

'Full of beans' was once used to describe a horse that was full of energy and in prime condition. The contribution made by the beans to the animal's excellent state of health is unclear; as a source of nourishment, beans may have been equated with energy and vitality. By the nineteenth century, the expression had moved from the stable to the dining room and people were similarly being described as 'full of beans' if they too were deemed to be in both good form and high spirits.

Getting your teeth into

'Getting your teeth into' something is a matter of literally 'getting to grips with it'. Whether you are 'getting your teeth into' a piece of work, a difficult problem, or a challenge of some sort, the allusion in this popular turn of phrase is to start 'chewing' and 'gnawing' at it in a determined and resolute manner.

Gilt off the gingerbread

Until the middle of the nineteenth century, stalls selling 'gingerbread', a cake mixed with treacle and flavoured with spices, were a common sight at fairs throughout the country. Often cut into shapes, such as the familiar 'gingerbread man', gingerbread was commonly decorated with gold leaf, or 'gilt', which although was sometimes genuine, in most cases was imitation. To take the 'gilt off the gingerbread' therefore was to reveal what it really was, which gave rise to the wider meaning of the expression – to show something up as worth far less than imagined, thereby destroying an illusion.

Gin

The distinctive taste of gin comes from the juice of the juniper berries used to flavour it. Juniper also gave the spirit the name by which it is now commonly known – the Old French word for 'juniper' was *genevre* (*genièvre* in modern French), which became known as 'geneva' in English and by the eighteenth century had been abbreviated to 'gin'.

Ginger up

The warm, piquant flavour that this popular spice lends to anything it is added to has resulted in the use of the word 'ginger' as a verb. The act of 'gingering up' someone means provoking them into activity, often by arousing anger and thereby raising their temperature.

Give the cold shoulder

The original 'cold shoulder' in this well-used turn of phrase was a rather bland cold shoulder of mutton, presented by the host for a guest who had outstayed their welcome. Whereas an appetizingly hot roast joint would customarily have greeted the guest on their arrival, the serving of a cold shoulder was a less appealing and none too subtle sign that it was time for them to leave. The meaning has subsequently extended beyond the code of hospitality – in its wider sense, 'giving the cold shoulder' means 'assuming a distant manner', which makes it clear that you want nothing to do with a particular individual.

Giving a basting

This use of 'basting' is in the sense of giving something a sound bashing or a beating. It is possible that it derives from the practice of medieval cooks in beating lazy scullions with the 'basting stick', which was used to pour hot fat from the dripping pan over the joint and other meats when roasting on the spit.

Giving beans

Meaning to 'give someone a thrashing', this old expression may be a straightforward translation of the French *S'il me donne des pois, je lui donnerai de fèves*, meaning 'If he gives me peas, I'll give him beans'. The sense is similar to the expression 'to return [something] with interest', in other words to repay blows with an even stronger buffeting.

GO
BANANAS

DURING THE TWENTIETH CENTURY 'GOING BANANAS' BECAME A WIDELY USED TERM FOR 'GOING CRAZY' OR 'EXCITED', OFTEN WITH VIOLENT REPERCUSSIONS. WHY BANANAS SHOULD BE CREDITED WITH THIS EFFECT IS UNCERTAIN, BUT THE APPARENT INSTABILITY OF SO-CALLED 'BANANA REPUBLICS' MAY HAVE HAD AN INFLUENCE. IN AUSTRALIA AND AMERICA, 'BANANA OIL' WAS USED COLLOQUIALLY TO MEAN 'NONSENSE'. THERE IS ALSO THE SUGGESTION THAT THE CURVED SHAPE OF THE BANANA, WHICH THUS DEVIATES FROM THE 'STRAIGHT' LINE, MAY HAVE BEEN AN INFLUENCE, JUST AS 'PEAR-SHAPED' HAS BECOME A POPULAR WAY OF REFERRING TO SOMETHING THAT HAS GONE BADLY WRONG.

Going to Tommy Dodd for drinks

The 'Tommy Dodd' in this expression refers to the 'odd man out', the person who loses the toss of a coin and drops out of a group. Although there may be several 'Tommy Dodds' in a group at the start, only two men are left tossing the coin to see who will pay for a round of drinks in the end. So 'going to Tommy Dodd for drinks' really means 'tossing a coin to see who will pay for the next round'.

Gone to pot

Possibly a shortened version of the mid-sixteenth-century phrase 'go to the pot', this expression meaning to be 'ruined' or 'no longer of use' refers to the chopped-up pieces of leftover meat and vegetables, which, in earlier times, would have been tossed into the cooking pot over the fire to be cooked and served as hash, the implication being that the original value of the food has been lost.

Gooseberry fool

A 'gooseberry fool' is a dessert made by crushing gooseberries through a sieve and mixing them with sugar and cream or custard. In this sense the 'fool' is an adaptation of the French *fouler*, meaning 'to crush'.

Grapes of wrath

Perhaps best known as the title of John Steinbeck's 1939 Pulitzer Prize-winning novel about the plight of dispossessed Oklahoma farming families, this phrase was taken from Julia Ward Howe's famous Civil War song 'The Battle Hymn of the American Republic' (1861): 'Mine eyes have seen the glory of the coming of the Lord: / He is trampling out the vintage where the grapes of wrath are stored'. This in turn was inspired by the biblical reference 'And the angel thrust in his sickle into the earth, and gathered the vine of the earth, and cast it into the great winepress of the wrath of God', found at the end of the fourteenth chapter of the Book of Revelations.

Greengage

In 1725, or thereabouts, Sir William Gage of Hengrove in Suffolk introduced a new, pale green, variety of plum into England from France, and the fruit was thus named 'greengage' in his honour. In France, the fruit has a more regal name, being known as *Reine Claude* (Queen Claude), in honour of Claude (1499-1524), queen consort of Francis I of France.

Grog

Due to the lack of fresh drinking water supplies at sea, from around the seventeenth century officers and men in the Royal Navy were issued with regular supplies of neat rum. While this may have helped to improve morale, perhaps not surprisingly, it did little to improve efficiency and discipline. In 1740, British naval officer Admiral Edward Vernon began issuing watered-down rum to the men under his command. Because of the cloak he habitually wore, which was made from grogram, a coarse material spun from silk and wool and stiffened with gum, the admiral was nicknamed the 'Old Grog', and before long the daily drink ration he had introduced acquired the same name. In time, 'grog' became more widely applied to all kinds of alcoholic beverages, and by the nineteenth century the term 'groggy', in the sense of 'shaky' and 'tottering,' was also well established.

Guinea fowl

The only connection between these birds and the English guinea coin, predominantly distributed in the eighteenth century, is that both the gold from which the coin was minted and the bird itself originated from Guinea in West Africa.

GUNS
BEFORE
BUTTER

THE POLITICAL CATCHPHRASE 'GUNS BEFORE BUTTER' BECAME CLOSELY ASSOCIATED WITH THE NAZI LEADERSHIP IN GERMANY IN THE 1930S, WHEN GOEBBELS, GOERING AND HESS ALL MADE USE OF IT IN ONE FORM OR ANOTHER, INSISTING THAT GERMANY NEEDED TO BE STRONGLY ARMED AS A NATION RATHER THAN TREATED TO THE LUXURIES OF LIFE. THE PHRASE HAS BEEN QUOTED SUBSEQUENTLY IN SITUATIONS IN WHICH A COUNTRY, PLACED ON A WAR FOOTING, HAS HAD TO FORSAKE EVEN SIMPLE PLEASURES, SUCH AS BUTTER, IN THE INTERESTS OF NATIONAL DEFENCE.

Half a loaf is better than no bread

Quoted by John Heywood in his *Dialogue of Proverbs* in 1546, this proverb is one of many that urge us to make the best of our lot and carries a clear message – if you can't get all that you want, try to be content with what you do manage to get; after all, something is always better than nothing.

Half-baked

Anything 'half-baked' is, by allusion to cooking bread, 'soft', 'unfinished' and 'incomplete'. As a consequence the term is widely used in the case of individuals whom some might describe as being 'soft in the head'. 'Half-baked' is also applied to propositions and ideas regarded as ill-conceived and not fully thought through.

Ham actor

Since the days of Shakespeare, the stage has had more than its fair share of 'ham actors' – indeed, a scene in *Hamlet* involves the prince giving the visiting players a few tips on how to avoid being just such an actor. It is possible that the first three letters of *Hamlet* may provide one explanation for the origin of the term, both because of the prince's thorough account of a ham actor's gestures and style of delivery, and because of the stage tradition that all actors labelled as 'has beens' have played Hamlet at some stage in their earlier careers. In nineteenth-century theatre, some actors removed their blackface make-up with ham fat – such actors being known as 'ham fatters' or 'hams' – and this practice has been suggested as another possible origin for the term. Although the exact root of the 'ham actor' may be uncertain, few would argue that Hamlet's description is as appropriate today as it was over 400 years ago in Shakespeare's time.

Hamburger

A flat patty of fried meat and onion, the 'hamburger' acquired its name in America having been brought to the New World by sailors from the north-west German port of Hamburg, around which beef had been prepared and eaten in this form for several hundred years. The word 'beefburger' was later coined in the food industry in the lame attempt to avoid any unlikely confusion between beef and ham.

Ham-fisted

To be 'ham-fisted' is to be 'clumsy'. The expression no doubt refers to hands that are shaped like hams and are therefore less than ideal for dextrous manual tasks.

Hard cheese

'Hard cheese', meaning 'tough luck', has a distinctively nineteenth-century ring and indeed was common among the officer class of the Victorian army. The allusion is obscure, though the unpalatable nature of cheese that has gone hard may convey something of the disappointment and sense of bad luck implicit in the phrase.

Hash

'Hash' is a dish made from leftovers, such as chopped-up meat, potatoes and vegetables, mixed together and cooked in a pan. It is lowly meal and as such has influenced the use of 'hash' in phrases including 'to make a hash of' something, meaning to 'make a mess' of it.

HEARD THROUGH
THE GRAPEVINE

NOWADAYS, NEWS SAID TO HAVE BEEN CARRIED ON THE 'GRAPEVINE' TENDS TO REFER TO HEARSAY AND RUMOUR, WHEREAS THE PHRASE WAS ORIGINALLY USED TO COMMUNICATE A VERY DEFINITE MESSAGE. THE EXPRESSION IS THOUGHT TO HAVE BEEN COINED DURING THE TIME WHEN THE ABOLITION OF SLAVERY WAS GATHERING MOMENTUM IN AMERICA. SUPPORTERS OF ABOLITION WOULD SUPPOSEDLY HANG LAUNDRY ON A CLOTHESLINE TO SIGNAL THE SECURITY SITUATION IN THEIR NEIGHBOURHOOD – ONE PARTICULAR SELECTION OF LAUNDRY INDICATED THAT IT WAS SAFE FOR RUNAWAY SLAVES TO MOVE IN THE AREA, ANOTHER WARNED THAT IT WAS DANGEROUS. SINCE ROPE WAS EXPENSIVE, GRAPEVINES WERE OFTEN SUBSTITUTED FOR CLOTHESLINES AND SO THE PRIMITIVE SIGNALLING SYSTEM BECAME KNOWN AS THE 'GRAPEVINE TELEGRAPH', LATER SHORTENED TO THE 'GRAPEVINE' ON ITS OWN.

He eats no fish

Current during the reign of Elizabeth I, this term was used to imply that a person was honest and trustworthy. Such an assertion was based on the fact that the person in question did not eat fish on Fridays, an action which distinguished Roman Catholics from Protestants, who refused to follow what was widely regarded as a Papist superstition.

Here we go gathering nuts in May

Since there are no nuts that can be gathered in May, this age-old children's rhyme is another example of how two words that sound similar can be confused. The line originally ran 'Here we go gathering knots of may', which referred to the time-honoured custom of gathering 'knots' of flowers on May Day.

High tea

'High tea' is an early evening meal that is more substantial than, and therefore elevated above, the customary afternoon 'tea' of dainty sandwiches and cakes, but offers less to eat than supper, which is served later in the evening.

Honeymoon

For followers of the old Germanic custom that required newly married couples to drink diluted honey during their first month of life together, the first thirty days of marriage were literally a period of 'sweetness' – the honey was later supplemented with mead, a sweet wine made from honey. Honeymoons were not, and are not, restricted to Germanic peoples, however. French couples begin their life together with a *lune de miel* ('moon of honey'), as do their Italian counterparts who enjoy a *luna di miele*.

Hooch

Coined in America as the slang for 'rough whisky' or other crudely distilled spirits, 'hooch' is an abbreviation of the Alaskan Indian *Hoochino*, the name of a tribe that brewed a liquor of this sort. The term became widely know during Prohibition (1920-33) but actually dates from the late nineteenth century.

Horseradish

The use of 'horse' as a prefix often denotes large size or coarseness, as in the terms horse chestnut, horseplay and horse laugh. With a larger and more pungent root than the normal radish, 'horseradish' is often used to make a piquant sauce, which is traditionally served with beef, rather than being eaten in its entirety like the ordinary radish, which is a common ingredient in summer salads. Traditionally, too, it was used in home remedies to cure ailments as diverse as rheumatism and coughs.

Hotchpotch

The French words *hocher*, meaning 'to shake', and *pot*, literally 'pot', provide the source for the term 'hotchpotch' in both its culinary and legal meanings. By the fifteenth century, 'hotchpotch' had become the name given to a thick broth made from a mixture of ingredients including meat, vegetables, condiments and anything else that the cook had to hand or cared to add. This gave rise to the wider meaning in which a 'hotchpotch' is a 'confused jumble' or muddle. As a legal term, 'hotchpotch' is a process involving the division of a fund or estate between a number of beneficiaries. If any party has already received a share, he or she may be asked to bring that share into 'hotchpotch', in other words to have it taken into consideration as part of the total fund, before individual shares can be apportioned.

Hot cross bun

Customarily eaten at Easter on Good Friday, 'hot cross buns' are traditionally marked with a cross to show that they have supposedly been made from the same dough as the bread of the holy Eucharist. The sacred nature of these fruited, spiced buns apparently accounted for the many examples of folklore and superstitions associated with them, such as the belief that a bun served on Good Friday would keep for a year without going mouldy. Indeed, it was once common practice to hang hot cross buns in the house to ward off evil spirits.

Hot dog

'Hot dogs' do not appear to have acquired their now universally recognized name until the beginning of the twentieth century. During the nineteenth century, hot sausages served in long rolls or buns had been sold by street vendors in America and long sausages, known as 'frankfurters' after the German city where they had originated, were particularly popular. Since their shape also resembled the long-bodied, short-legged breed of German dog the dachshund, the sausages became known as 'hot dachshund sausages', which proved to be a bit of mouthful in every respect. It was the sports cartoonist T.A. Dorgan, known to his fans as TAD, who took the final step and started referring to the hot sausage in a roll as a 'hot dog' and almost immediately the name superseded all others.

How many beans make five

An abbreviated form of 'he knows how many beans make five', this age-old phrase refers to the practice of moving beans around when counting, as in an abacus, the implication being that only the sharp-witted will produce the right answer and that the person is therefore 'no fool'. Of course, everyone knows that five beans make five, but how about the trick version of the question, 'how many blue beans make five white beans'? And the answer? Five blue beans make five white ones – but only if they are peeled!

HUMBLE
PIE

THE FOOD SERVED AT A MEDIEVAL HUNTING FEAST ESTABLISHED A MARKED SOCIAL DISTINCTION BETWEEN DINERS. THE LORD, HIS FAMILY AND GUESTS WOULD BE SERVED VENISON AT THE HIGH TABLE, WHILE, FURTHER DOWN THE TABLE, THOSE OF LESSER STANDING, INCLUDING THE HUNTSMEN AND RETAINERS, WERE FED A PIE MADE OF THE DEER'S HEART, LIVER AND ENTRAILS, OTHERWISE KNOWN AS 'UMBLES'. 'HUMBLE PIE', THEREFORE, IS A PUN ON 'UMBLE PIE', AND THOSE PRESENTED WITH IT ARE REQUIRED, METAPHORICALLY, TO EAT INFERIOR FOOD IN AN INFERIOR POSITION, THUS TO 'EAT HUMBLE PIE' MEANS TO COME DOWN FROM THE LOFTY POSITION THAT HAS WRONGLY BEEN ASSUMED IN ORDER TO DEFER TO OTHERS – FREQUENTLY THOSE THAT HAD PREVIOUSLY BEEN LOOKED DOWN UPON.

I have eggs on the spit

Cooking eggs on a spit was a particularly time-consuming process in medieval cookery, requiring the cook's constant attention. The eggs first had to be boiled, then the yolks were removed to be mixed with spices before being replaced back inside the whites. Following this, they were fed onto a spit and roasted over the fire. With so much to attend to, the cook had no time for anything else. Despite the fact that cooking over a spit is a lost art, and indeed the fact that many people have never even heard of roasted eggs, this activity gave rise to the current use of the expression 'I have eggs on the spit', meaning 'I am too busy to do anything else'.

I should cocoa

The expression 'I should cocoa' is less frequently used today than it once was, though its meaning remains 'Certainly not!' The origin of this curious saying lies in rhyming slang, in which 'cocoa' is the abbreviated form of 'coffee and cocoa', meaning 'I should hope so!' In this case, however, it is used ironically to mean the exact opposite.

IF YOU CAN'T STAND THE

HEAT,

GET OUT OF THE KITCHEN

PLAIN-SPEAKING HARRY S. TRUMAN, THE THIRTY-THIRD PRESIDENT OF THE UNITED STATES OF AMERICA WHO HELD OFFICE FROM 1945–53, COINED A NUMBER OF MEMORABLE DOWN-TO-EARTH MAXIMS, OF WHICH THIS BECAME ONE OF THE MOST WIDELY USED. AS HE WROTE IN HIS AUTOBIOGRAPHICAL BOOK *MR CITIZEN* (1960), 'I USED TO HAVE A SAYING THAT APPLIES HERE, AND I NOTE THAT SOME PEOPLE HAVE PICKED IT UP: "IF YOU CAN'T STAND THE HEAT, GET OUT OF THE KITCHEN".' THE ALLUSION TO SLAVING OVER A HOT STOVE, WHILE UNDER PRESSURE TO PREPARE A MEAL, IS WELL APPLIED TO OTHER SITUATIONS IN THE SENSE OF 'IF YOU CAN'T TAKE THE STRAIN, DON'T GET INVOLVED'.

In a jam

Although spelt the same as the fruit conserve commonly known as 'jam', the word in this expression has been recorded since the eighteenth century in the sense of 'to press' or 'squeeze tightly'. As a noun, a 'jam' in this context is the result of being pressed or squeezed, usually into a situation that is not of one's choosing.

In a pickle

References to being 'in a pickle' date back to the time of Shakespeare and all are applied with the sense of being 'in a predicament' or 'in a sorry plight'. From the fourteenth century, a 'pickle' was a brine in which food was preserved. Perhaps the unpleasant taste of this salt liquor led to the origin of the phrase, which has been current for over 400 years.

In a stew

The allusion of 'a state of anxiety' to being 'in a stew' dates from nineteenth-century slang. This may be due to the agitated state in which the contents of a stew are cooked combined with the perspiration that can be caused when people 'in a stew' become over-heated.

In meal or in malt

Millers were frequently regarded with suspicion by their neighbours, who were often convinced that they took more than their fair share of the harvest when it passed through their hands. This underlying doubt about a miller's conduct and honesty gave rise to the saying 'in meal or in malt'. Since meal and malt were both end products of milled grain, either had the potential to produce a profit, and as the miller was entitled to a share of the proceeds as his payment he would benefit 'in one way or another', or figuratively 'in meal or in malt', whatever the grain was used for.

IT'S NO USE CRYING OVER SPILT MILK

AS EARLY AS 1659, THIS PROVERB WAS RECORDED AS 'NO WEEPING FOR SHED MILK' AND IT IS LIKELY THAT IT WAS IN USE EVEN EARLIER THAN THAT. THE ALLUSION TO THE DAIRY AND KITCHEN IS SELF-EVIDENT: MILK, ONCE SPILT, IS WASTED AND CANNOT BE RETRIEVED. IN THE SAME WAY, ONCE A MISFORTUNE HAS OCCURRED IT CANNOT BE REMEDIED. WE MIGHT ALSO SAY, THAT 'YOU CAN'T TURN BACK THE CLOCK'.

Jerked beef

'Jerked beef' consists of beef cut into strips and dried in the sun. The term entered English in the eighteenth century as the Anglicized form of the South American word *charqui* for meat preserved in this way.

Junket

'Junket' started life in the fourteenth century as a rush basket for carrying fish. By the following century it had become a dish prepared with curdled cream, which was laid on a bed of rushes. Another century later, 'junket' had moved upmarket to become a dainty dish or confection served at feasts and banquets. From there it was only a short move to apply 'junket' to the festivity itself, frequently one that comprises some form of outing.

Just the cheese

Anything described as being 'just the cheese' could equally be called 'just the thing', for 'cheese' in this sense is borrowed from the Persian and Urdu word *chiz*, meaning 'thing'. The English use of the word originated in India, where it acquired the familiar spelling 'cheese'. Once incorporated into the English language, the expression became associated with native cheeses, giving rise to expressions of enthusiastic approval such as 'that's prime Stilton!'.

Keep the pot boiling

For a long time, to 'keep the pot boiling' implied earning money to keep the
family in food and this sense is maintained in 'potboiler', a term which is often
applied to books and other literary works of limited artistic merit that are
written primarily to make money. However, 'keeping the pot boiling' also means
maintaining interest in a project or task to ensure that initial enthusiasm does
not flag.

Keep your pecker up

The tendency to hang one's head low when unhappy or anxious often invites
encouragement from others to remain cheerful by 'keeping your pecker up'.
'Pecker' here refers to the mouth and by association the face and head in general.
'Keep your pecker up' therefore literally means to lift the head, thereby adopting
a more confident stance and is used in a figurative sense to mean 'stay cheerful';
'keep your chin up' has the same meaning.

Killing the fatted calf

This expression, meaning 'to celebrate' and 'to welcome with the best of everything', derives from the parable of the prodigal son in the New Testament, in which Christ tells the story of two brothers, the elder of whom remains at home, working diligently, while his younger brother takes his share of his inheritance and leaves home to squander it. In time, the younger brother sees the error of his ways and returns home in due humility to ask his father for forgiveness and to be allowed back, even if in the capacity of a farm labourer. So overjoyed is the father to see his son again that he offers him presents and arranges a welcoming feast, which necessitates 'killing the fatted calf' usually kept for important celebrations. The elder brother, however, resents the reception his brother has received until his father explains, in the words of the gospel, 'Son, thou art ever with me, and all that I have is thine. It was meet that we should make merry, and be glad: for this thy brother was dead, and is alive again; and was lost, and is found.'

Knowing which side your bread is buttered

Since the sixteenth century, the phrase 'knowing which side your bread is buttered' has been used to mean knowing and recognizing where your own interests lie.

Knowing your onions

This well-used saying alludes to the idea that peeling the closely packed layers of an onion is akin to the intricate study and understanding of a complex issue or problem. To 'know your onions' has therefore come to mean that you are highly proficient and know your subject inside out.

Lager beer

In German *Lager* means 'store' and *lagerbier* is therefore 'beer for storing', in other words beer that should mature in the barrel before being consumed. The English usage of 'lager' and the less common 'lager beer' are direct borrowings from German.

Lamb's wool

Made to a traditional recipe of juice from apples that have been roasted in ale, sugar and nutmeg, the drink 'lamb's wool' is soft on the palate and probably acquired its name from the association with the softness of a lamb's wool.

Land of milk and honey

The biblical origin of this expression has led to its figurative use in denoting the blessings of heaven. A 'land of milk and honey' is one of great fertility in which nourishing and plentiful food can be produced. The phrase comes from the Book of Exodus, where God tells Moses of the land to which he will lead the children of Israel from captivity in Egypt: 'And I am come down to deliver them out of the hand of the Egyptians, and to bring them up out of that land unto a good land and a large, unto a land flowing with milk and honey.'

LARDER

THE IMPORTANCE OF THE PIG IN THE DIET OF OUR ANCESTORS IS REVEALED IN THE ORIGIN OF THE WORD 'LARDER', WHICH NOW REFERS TO A ROOM OR CUPBOARD FOR STORING PROVISIONS IN GENERAL. 'LARDER' WAS COINED SOME TIME BEFORE THE FOURTEENTH CENTURY FROM THE LATIN *LARIDUM* (SOMETIMES *LARDUM*), MEANING 'THE FAT OF BACON' AND HERE THE CLOSE ASSOCIATION WITH THE PIG BECOMES EVIDENT. THE FIRST 'LARDERS' WERE PRINCIPALLY USED TO STORE PIG MEAT IN VARIOUS FORMS – ONLY MUCH LATER WERE OTHER PRESERVED FOODS INCLUDED IN THE MEANING. UNTIL THEN THE PIG PROVIDED THE LARGEST SHARE OF PRESERVED AND SALTED MEAT.

Leg-of-mutton sleeve

Triangular in shape, narrow at the cuff and flaring to the point where it joins the main body of the garment between the shoulder and the waist, a 'leg-of-mutton sleeve' is, as its name suggests, reminiscent of a leg of lamb, or mutton.

Lemon sole

This flatfish owes its name to the French word *limande*, meaning literally a 'flat board', which through English usage became 'lemon', thereby losing the visual significance of the French and introducing a citrus fruit with which the origin of the fish in fact has no connection.

Life is just a bowl of cherries

A song from the American musical *George White's Scandals* of 1931, 'Life is Just a Bowl of Cherries' was written by Lew Brown with music by Ray Henderson, and popularized by Ethel Merman, who helped establish the title as the proverbial expression that 'everything is wonderful'.

Limeys

From the beginning of the nineteenth century, British sailors received a free issue of lime or lemon juice at sea to help protect them from scurvy. This led to the nickname 'Lime-juicers', abbreviated to 'Limeys', by which Britons were known in America and later Australia.

Living high off the hog

This expression alludes to the popular opinion that the choicest cuts of meat on a pig, which at one time was the principal source of meat for most of the population, are found on the back and on the upper part of the leg, while the poorer quality meat is to be found lower down. To 'live high off the hog' therefore means to live in an affluent or extravagant manner.

Lobster

For centuries, 'Lobster' was the nickname given to British soldiers, an allusion to the fact that lobsters change colour and become red when cooked in the same way that a man recruited into the army 'changed colour' when he donned his uniform and became a 'redcoat'. During the seventeenth century, the nickname was also given to certain troops who wore 'lobster-tail' helmets that were fitted with overlapping plates which protected the back of the wearers' necks.

Lobster Newberg

Delmonico's was *the* fashionable restaurant in late nineteenth-century New York and it was here that Lobster Newberg was first served. The recipe, in which lobster is cooked in a thick, creamy sauce flavoured with brandy, sherry, or wine, with paprika or cayenne pepper and egg yolks, was, so the story goes, initially named 'Lobster Wenberg' after Ben Wenberg, a sea-captain and regular patron who supplied the cayenne pepper and introduced the original South American dish to Delmonico's. The recipe would still be named after him had he not fallen out with the proprietor, Charles Delmonico, who took revenge by removing the dish from the menu. However, after several customers complained, the dish was reinstated as 'Lobster Newberg', a crude anagram of Wenberg's name, thereby consigning his memory to culinary oblivion.

Long spoon to sup with the Devil

This proverb has been recorded since the end of the fourteenth century when Chaucer referred to it in *The Squire's Tale* as part of his renowned work the *Canterbury Tales*. The meaning is a warning to 'use caution when dealing with dangerous people'.

Looking for a needle in a bottle of hay

Since hay is not a commodity usually associated with bottles, this expression is easy to misinterpret at first glance. However, the 'bottle' used in this sense was known in English by the fourteenth century and is the Anglicized form of the Old French *botel*, which is the diminutive of *botte*, meaning 'a bundle'. Thus 'looking for a needle in a bottle of hay' means 'looking for a needle in a bundle of hay', or, as the version now more commonly used puts it, 'looking for a needle in a haystack', implying that something is extremely difficult to find.

Lose in hake, but gain in herring

Hake prey on herring and because of this they used to be driven away from herring fishing grounds. Although fishermen thereby lost the chance to catch hake, they profited from the large stocks of herring which remained. Therefore to 'lose in hake, but gain in herring' is to 'lose one way, but gain in another'.

Loving cup

The 'loving cup' forms part of the dining customs in many long-established institutions, such as university colleges and City guilds. The principal of sharing a cup of wine originated in pagan times – the traditional wassail bowl is one such primitive custom that has survived – and was later adopted by the monasteries to serve Christianity in the form of the *poculum caritatis*, or 'loving cup', a large vessel filled with wine, which was passed from drinker to drinker as a mark of unity and fellowship bearing similarities to the Eucharist. Present-day custom often involves the use of a two-handled vessel, which is passed around the company at special dinners. Tradition frequently dictates that two people, seated next to each other, stand when the 'loving cup' reaches them – one to drink from the cup, the other to act as his 'defender'. Once the drinker has taken his or her share, the cup is then passed to the 'defender', who drinks while being 'defended' by the adjacent diner. This continues until all those present have taken part in the ritual.

LUNCH

THE WORD 'LUNCH' WAS PROBABLY USED IN ENGLISH BEFORE ITS LONGER FORM 'LUNCHEON', THOUGH BOTH HAVE BEEN RECORDED SINCE THE SIXTEENTH CENTURY. TO BEGIN WITH, 'LUNCH' REFERRED TO A 'THICK PIECE' OR 'HUNK' OF FOOD AND PROBABLY ORIGINATED FROM THE SPANISH *LONGA*, MEANING A 'SLICE'. 'LUNCHEON' MAY WELL HAVE BEEN DERIVED AS A SIMPLE EXTENSION OF 'LUNCH' IN THE SAME WAY THAT 'TRUNCHEON' WAS AN EXTENSION OF AN EARLIER AND SHORTER WORD.

Macaroni

One of the earliest forms of pasta, the thin wheaten tubes called 'macaroni' gained their name from the Greek word *makaria*, meaning 'barley food'. In the mid-eighteenth century the name was appropriated by a group of fashionable young men known as dandies who introduced *macaroni* to London dining tables from their European travels and styled themselves the Macaroni Club.

Mackerel sky

A 'mackerel sky', the layer of mottled cloud that resembles the colour and patina of a mackerel's skin, is a well-known forerunner of rain, though usually a shower rather than a heavy storm. The expression is widely used in weatherlore, for example in the forecasting rhyme, 'A mackerel sky won't last twenty-four hours dry'.

Madeleine

The nineteenth-century French pastry cook Madeleine Paulmier may well have inspired the name of the small fancy sponge cake, traditionally baked in scallop-shaped moulds, that is now called a 'madeleine'.

MARMALADE

IN PORTUGUESE, *MARMELADA* IS 'QUINCE JAM' (FROM *MARMELO*, THE PORTUGUESE FOR 'QUINCE'). ONCE ORANGES HAD BECOME A COMMON FRUIT IN EUROPE, THE ENGLISH NAME WAS TRANSFERRED TO WHAT WAS EFFECTIVELY 'ORANGE JAM'; IN EUROPE *MARMELADE* STILL REFERS TO 'JAM' IN GENERAL. IT WAS ONLY AT THE VERY END OF THE EIGHTEENTH CENTURY THAT THE FIRST MODERN 'MARMALADE' WAS MADE IN DUNDEE, SCOTLAND.

Mayonnaise

This popular condiment was originally named *mahonnaise* after the port of Mahon in Minorca. The island was captured by the French in 1756 and, on going ashore, the commander of the French forces demanded something to eat. With nothing to hand but oil, vinegar, egg yolks and seasoning, his chef beat these together and created the first 'mayonnaise'.

Mealy-mouthed

In German the expression *Mehl im Maule behalten* translates as 'to carry meal in the mouth', meaning 'lacking straightforwardness in speech'. This may well have influenced the origin of the English term 'mealy-mouthed', which is used to describe a person who is 'velvet-tongued', 'unwilling to give offence' and 'hypocritical'.

Melba toast

Made from very thin slices of bread, or from bread which is first toasted, then sliced laterally and toasted again, this crisp and dry form of toast was devised in 1897 by the great chef Auguste Escoffier. It was created for Dame Nellie Melba, the renowned Australian operatic soprano, when she was unwell, and was named after her.

Mercury fig

In ancient Rome the first fig gathered from a fig tree was devoted to the god Mercury. In Latin, it was known as the *Ficus ad Mercurium*. From this, the English proverbial term 'Mercury fig' has come to be applied to all first fruits and first works.

Milk run

During the Second World War, Royal Air Force crews referred to the regular sorties flown day after day as 'milk runs'. The allusion is to the daily doorstep delivery of milk, which becomes a routine for milkmen who do the same round day in, day out.

Milky Way

In Greek *gala* means 'milk' and since the fourteenth century 'galaxy', one of the words in English derived from *gala*, has been applied to the group of stars that are known as the Milky Way, which appears to circle the night sky with a milky film of light.

Mint

A common garden plant and a herb with many uses from the traditional mint sauce to refreshing summer drinks, mint has ancient origins. In Roman mythology Minthe was a nymph beloved of Pluto, god of the underworld. Pluto's wife, Prosperine, who was jealous of Minthe, changed her into a herb, which is said to have borne her name ever since. In Latin this became *menta*, from which came the French *menthe* and the modern English 'mint'.

Money for jam

Sweet, tasty and nourishing, 'jam' has long been given the colloquial meaning of something that is either particularly pleasant, or which is obtained with very little difficulty. Hence the use of 'money for jam' for an unexpected stroke of luck, or a sum of money acquired with little effort.

MOUNTAIN
DEW

IN THE SECOND HALF OF THE EIGHTEENTH CENTURY, SMALL-SCALE DISTILLING OF WHISKY WAS BANNED IN SCOTLAND. DEMAND FOR THE SPIRIT REMAINED AS STRONG AS EVER, HOWEVER, AND ILLICIT STILLS HIDDEN AWAY IN THE MOUNTAINS BECAME THE ONLY SOURCE OF WHISKY FOR MANY HIGHLANDERS, LEADING TO THE TERM 'MOUNTAIN DEW', WHICH HAS BEEN USED TO REFER TO ILLICITLY DISTILLED SPIRITS EVER SINCE.

Muffin

The soft, spongy texture of a 'muffin' may account for the origin of its name. In Old French, *pain moufflet* was a type of soft bread, and this term may have become corrupted in its translation to English.

Mustard gas

Dichlorodiethyl sulphide is a colourless oily liquid with a faint small of garlic and mustard. Released into the atmosphere, it produces a vapour that raises blisters on human skin. During the First World War, mustard gas was one of the most feared early examples of modern chemical warfare.

Mutton

The word 'mutton', like 'beef', reflects the social hierarchy in England following the Norman Conquest. The Old French *moton* ('sheep') came, in English, to mean the flesh, the meat eaten by the Norman overlords while their Saxon herdsmen looked after the animals.

Mutton-chop whiskers

Shaved narrow at the temples and then extending down in a triangular form to the jawline, 'mutton-chop whiskers' are so-called because their shape resembles that of a mutton chop.

Mutton dressed as lamb

This is a derogatory reference to an older woman who dresses to make herself appear younger than she evidently is. In days gone by 'mutton' was slang for a 'prostitute', which may also have had a bearing on the derivation of the expression.

Nappy ale

Not the secret tipple of nanny in the nursery as the expression might lead one to suppose, 'nappy ale' was actually used in the eighteenth and nineteenth centuries to describe a strong ale that had a froth, or *nap*, when it was poured.

Nectar

'Nectar' was the drink of the gods in Greek mythology, which, alongside their food 'ambrosia', ensured immortality – the word 'nectar' is a compound of the Greek prefix *nek*, meaning 'death', and the suffix *-tar*, which has the sense of 'triumphing over'. Thus 'nectar' was a drink that 'triumphed over death' and as such was endowed with a delicious sweet taste. In this way, 'nectar' came to refer to any delicious drink. Similarly, the 'nectarine' was given its name because it was regarded as tasting 'as sweet as nectar'.

Neither barrel the better herring

This is one of several expressions that share a common meaning, 'much of a muchness' and 'six of one and half-a-dozen of the other' being two of the most common. All imply that two things are so similar that it is virtually impossible to draw a distinction between them. In this case the allusion is to two barrels of herring, which are of such similar quality and quantity that there is nothing to choose between them.

Neither fish, flesh, nor fowl

'Fish', 'flesh' and 'fowl' had specific social references in the Middle Ages: fish was the food of the priest, flesh the food of the people in general and fowl all that the poor could afford. Therefore something that was 'neither fish, flesh nor fowl', was not suitable for any class of people and by extension inappropriate in any given circumstances.

Nest egg

Used to describe a sum of money that has been saved for the future, this expression alludes to the common practice of placing an egg in a hen's nest to encourage her to lay, the implication being that even a small amount of money put away stimulates larger savings.

Nip

Nowadays, the suggestion of a 'nip' of something usually brings to mind a small quantity of whisky, but in the eighteenth century, when the word became established in English, it referred to a measure of wine or beer of half a pint or less. This was originally called a 'nipperkin', which was related to the Dutch *nippen* of similar meaning.

Not for all the tea in China

'Not for all the tea in China' became a popular hyperbole meaning 'under no circumstances' or 'not for any consideration' from the early part of the twentieth century. The expression is believed to have originated in Australia before spreading across the English-speaking world.

Not my cup of tea

This expression has a similar vintage to 'not for all the tea in China' and, genteel as it may appear, has an unequivocal note of censure that something is 'not to my liking'.

Not worth a fig

The 'fig' referred to in this expression is evidently something of very little value, which suggests that it is more likely to be the coarse hand gesture known as the 'fig of Spain', rather than the tasty fruit of the fig tree. The 'fig of Spain', also known as the 'fico', was well known in Elizabethan England – Shakespeare makes several references to it in his plays – and was formed by poking the thumb between the first and second fingers. Something that is 'not worth a fig' is therefore not worth anything at all.

Nutty as a fruitcake

The combined association of 'nuts' with being 'daft' and their use in rich fruitcakes gave rise to this turn of phrase, which implies that the person described as 'nutty as a fruitcake' is well and truly 'bonkers'. The 'nut' has been hard done by in the field of mental health. Perhaps its shape and consistency (a hard shell enclosing a softer centre) drew obvious parallels with the head – hence to be 'off one's nuts' or 'nuts' meant that you were 'crazy' or 'demented'. Similarly, a lunatic asylum was often referred to by the slang term 'nuthouse'.

Off his noodle

'Noodle' has been used to describe a 'simpleton' since the middle of the eighteenth century. The derivation of the name is vague, but 'off his noodle' is probably a reference to the older word 'noddle', slang for 'head' from at least the middle of the sixteenth century. In this way anyone who was 'off his noodle' was 'off his head' and therefore crazy.

Old bean

This good-natured greeting of familiarity, usually from one male to another, is similar in style to the more familiar 'old chap' and 'old man' and was particularly popular during the 1920s.

Old salt

An 'old salt' is a long-serving sailor – one who has been well 'salted' by his years spent at sea.

On tap

This phrase derives from the fact that in order to draw off liquor stored in a cask or barrel, a tap would have to be driven into the side. At first, 'on tap' applied solely to liquor available for immediate consumption, but in time the expression came to be used in a general context to mean anything, and indeed anyone, ready for immediate use.

ON THE
BACK
BURNER

IT IS ONLY IN THE LAST SIXTY YEARS OR SO, AFTER THE WIDESPREAD ARRIVAL OF ELECTRIC AND GAS COOKERS WITH MULTIPLE HOBS, THAT THE PHRASE 'ON THE BACK BURNER' HAS BECOME COMMONLY USED. IT MADE SENSE FOR COOKS TO PLACE PANS WITH SLOW-COOKING INGREDIENTS ON THE BURNERS AT THE BACK OF THE COOKER, THEREBY KEEPING THE BURNERS AT THE FRONT FREE FOR DISHES THAT COOK MORE QUICKLY AND THEREFORE REQUIRE GREATER ATTENTION. BEFORE LONG, 'ON THE BACK BURNER' CAME TO BE WIDELY USED AS AN INDICATION OF SOMETHING OF 'LOW PRIORITY'.

Other fish to fry

The phrase 'other fish to fry' dates back to the seventeenth century in the English language and is used as a way of saying that a person has other, usually better, things to be getting on with. The allusion to frying fish may be connected with the need to eat fish straight from the pan, in order for the dish to be enjoyed to the full. The act of 'frying fish' therefore implied setting time aside to prepare and eat it without interruption.

Out of the frying pan into the fire

Moving 'out of the frying pan into the fire' amounts to moving from one 'hot spot' to another and by implication from one bad situation into one equally as bad. The expression was current in English by the sixteenth century and similar turns of phrase are found in other languages; in ancient Greece, for instance, they talked of getting 'out of the smoke and into the flame'.

Out of the parsley bed

For around 200 years, between the seventeenth and nineteenth centuries, 'out of the parsley bed' was used to describe a 'love child', on the basis that parsley was considered to be an aphrodisiac.

Peaches and cream

At the turn of the twentieth century, a 'peaches and cream' complexion was the hallmark of feminine beauty as advertised and promoted by toiletry and cosmetic manufacturers. The delicate powdery bloom of the peach's skin complemented by a pale creamy colour was regarded as the epitome of healthy living and the 'look' to which all would-be 'beauties' aspired.

Peach Melba

This classic dessert, which combines peaches and raspberry sauce with vanilla ice cream, was invented by celebrated French chef Auguste Escoffier at London's Savoy Hotel in around 1892–3 in honour of the acclaimed Australian opera singer Dame Nellie Melba.

Pear-shaped

There are two current uses for the term 'pear-shaped': one physical, the other metaphorical. The first is an all too apt description of the consequences of middle-age spread, when the lower portions of the human torso start to become bigger than the upper, and is often applied to the female body shape, which has a natural tendency to be wider at the hip than the shoulder. In its figurative sense, 'pear-shaped' is applied to situations that have got out of control or gone awry.

Pea-soup fog

The traditional English soup made from dried peas tends to have a dull yellow colour and a thick consistency, both of which applied to the thick fogs and 'smogs' that were a feature of winters in towns and cities in days gone by. The association has persisted and the term 'pea-soup fog', or simply 'pea-souper', is still used to describe a very dense fog.

Peppercorn rent

Nominal rents of negligible value are sometimes paid by tenants who are allowed to occupy premises owned by others almost free of charge. These are referred to as 'peppercorn rents' since a peppercorn, though of very little value, still represents a financial exchange between the tenant and landlord, which is important because it confirms the owner's ultimate rights to the property. The term has been used since the Middle Ages, when a peppercorn had slightly more value than it does today but was still recognized as being of no appreciable worth.

Peppery

Anyone described as being 'peppery' might also be called 'hot-blooded', 'irascible' or 'easily roused'. Here the sense of 'spirited' is less than flattering than in the case of 'pepping up' (below); far from benefiting from associating with a 'peppery' individual, he – for a 'peppery person' is invariably male – is best avoided.

Pepping up

'Pep' has been used as an abbreviation for 'pepper' since the middle of the nineteenth century in phrases such as 'full of pep', 'to pep up', 'pep talk' and 'pep pill'. In every case the pungent, piquant effect of pepper has been applied figuratively in the sense of 'stimulating' and adding 'spirit'.

PHEASANT

IN THE ANCIENT WORLD, PHASIS WAS A RIVER IN THE LAND OF COLCHIS, AT THE EASTERN EDGE OF THE BLACK SEA IN WHAT IS PRESENT-DAY GEORGIA. IT WAS HERE THAT JASON AND THE ARGONAUTS SAILED IN THEIR QUEST FOR THE GOLDEN FLEECE. ACCORDING TO LEGEND, THEY FOUND BIRDS WITH LONG TAILS AND COLOURFUL PLUMAGE IN THE LAND AROUND PHASIS AND BROUGHT SOME BACK WITH THEM WHEN THEY RETURNED TO GREECE. THE PHASIAN BIRD THEN SPREAD WESTWARDS TO THE REST OF EUROPE. THE ROMANS KNEW IT AS *PHASIANUS*, WHILE IN OLD FRENCH IT WAS CALLED *FAISAN*, WHICH BECAME 'PHEASANT' IN ENGLISH.

Piece of cake

One of many wartime sayings that has entered the language, the Royal Air Force appears to have been responsible for coining this expression, although it had become widely used in many walks of life by the end of the Second World War. Its meaning – that something is 'easy' and 'can be done with little effort' – is obscure, but the reference may be to the simple act of eating cake. On the other hand, the phrase 'you can't have your cake and eat it', could well have played a part in its evolution – the inference here is that you can't have things both ways. Regardless of the precise origin, in either instance 'cake' is evidently something to be desired.

Piecrust table

Tables with intricately carved edges have been called 'piecrust tables' since the turn of the twentieth century. Originally dating from the eighteenth century, they are usually small, round, three-legged tables, with a raised, scalloped edge, from which tea and coffee were often served. The reference is to the decorative, crimped finish applied to the edge of piecrusts before they are baked in the oven.

Pie-eyed

'Pie-eyed' became popular slang for being well and truly drunk in the early years of the twentieth century, and is still used, and commonly understood, today. Most people in an advanced state of intoxication have difficulty seeing clearly and in an effort to focus tend to open their eyes wider, making them appear rounder than usual. Presumably it was this effect that led to the phrase being adopted as an apt description for someone who was suffering from the effects of drinking too much.

Pie in the sky

Coined by the itinerant labourer Joe Hill in America in 1911 as part of his militant Trade Union song book, *Songs of the Workers*, this phrase formed part of a trenchant political and social message, and featured in the chorus of 'The Preacher and the Slave': 'You will eat, bye and bye, / In that glorious land above the sky; / Work and pray, live on hay, / You'll get pie in the sky when you die.' Since then, 'pie in the sky' has meant the 'good time' or the 'good things' that are promised but which never come, or are never realized.

Playing gooseberry

There seem to be a couple of possible explanations for the origin of this otherwise obscure phrase applied to a chaperone, or other third party, who makes an awkward threesome while two lovers are romantically occupied. The chaperone was there, of course, for the sake of propriety and may have tactfully spent the time picking gooseberries, to allow the lovers a degree of privacy. On the other hand, anyone 'playing gooseberry' feels foolish and the association with a 'fool' may have led to the punning connection with 'gooseberry fool', the origin of which is described earlier.

Plonk

This much-used word, generally used nowadays to describe most cheap wine, was coined by British troops fighting in France during the First Wold War, who, on encountering French white wine, soon substituted the word 'plonk' for *vin blanc* (white wine). Since that time, English speakers have been knocking back plonk of every colour from wine-producing countries all over the world.

Ploughman's lunch

A midday meal of bread, cheese and pickle may have been the traditional meal for farm workers labouring in the fields for hundreds of years, but the name 'ploughman's lunch' was in fact only coined in the 1970s when the English County Cheese Council came up with it as a new advertising slogan. The phrase perfectly captured the spirit of 'old England' fostered by public houses in towns and cities as well as the countryside, and before long the 'ploughman's lunch', later 'ploughman's' on its own, was a permanent feature of the English pub menu.

Pork

In Old English, *pigga* or *picga* was the name given to what we now call a 'pig'. In ancient Rome, however, a 'pig' was known by the Latin *porcus*, which became *porc* in Old French. Following the Norman Conquest, the distinction between 'pig' and 'pork' became another indication of the social division between Normans and Saxons, similar to that seen with 'beef' and 'mutton'. The Norman word *porc* was used for the flesh of the animal, which the Normans were served at table. Their Saxon servants, on the other hand, retained the name 'pig', since their contact was invariably with the live animal which they tended for their Norman masters.

Potatoes and point

When times were hard and there was nothing to eat but potatoes, children were told to point the potatoes on their plates towards imaginary extras, such as meat, cheese and seasoning, and then eat them. This gave rise to the expression 'potatoes and point', which alludes to a very meagre meal.

Pot calling the kettle black

Until cooking stoves and ranges became common kitchen fittings, all cooking vessels had to be heated over open fires. This inevitably led to their being blackened by the flames, as alluded to in this long-standing expression, which cautions against criticizing others for faults you have yourself.

Potluck

The pot referred to here is that which was traditionally kept simmering over a kitchen fire, where any leftovers would be put to bubble away as a thick stew to be served at mealtimes. Inviting visitors to take 'potluck' thus implied asking them to join in with eating whatever happened to be in the pot, rather than expecting a specially prepared meal. In its broader meaning the phrase equates to 'taking a chance'.

Potpourri

The literal translation of the French *potpourri* is 'rotten pot', which scarcely does justice to the delightful fragrance created by the selection of sweet-smelling flower petals and herbs from which a potpourri is traditionally made. 'Potpourri' occurs in both French and English in the sense of a musical 'medley' and it still retains an earlier meaning in French as a type of meat stew.

Proof of the pudding

In its full wording this old proverb runs 'the proof of the pudding is in the eating', with 'proof ' in this case meaning 'test' rather than its normal sense of 'verifying that something is true'. The expression was first recorded in the fourteenth century and its meaning is that just as tasting a pudding, rather than looking at it, is the only way to judge it, so performance, not appearances, is the only true test of a person's claims or ability.

PULLING THE CHESTNUTS OUT OF THE FIRE

SINCE THE MIDDLE AGES, 'PULLING THE CHESTNUTS OUT OF THE FIRE' HAS BEEN USED IN THE SENSE OF RETRIEVING A DIFFICULT SITUATION FOR SOMEONE, OFTEN BY EXTRICATING THEM FROM A DIFFICULT SITUATION OR SPARING THEM EMBARRASSMENT. THE ALLUSION IN THE SAYING IS TO THE ANCIENT FABLE OF THE MONKEY AND THE CAT. SEEING CHESTNUTS ROASTING IN THE EMBERS OF A FIRE, THE MONKEY DECIDES HE WOULD LIKE TO EAT THEM. HOWEVER, BECAUSE REMOVING THE HOT CHESTNUTS WOULD MEAN BURNING HIMSELF, HE PERSUADES HIS FRIEND THE CAT TO USE HIS PAWS TO PULL THE CHESTNUTS FROM THE FIRE FOR HIM.

Punch

According to the *Account of East India* written in 1698, the beverage that became popularly known as 'punch' acquired its name from *panch*, the number 'five' in several Indian languages, which referred to the five ingredients from which the drink was traditionally made: spirits, water, spice, sugar and some form of acidic fruit juice. The word 'puncheon', however, meaning a large cask, often a container for wine, had already been in use in English by the fifteenth century and 'punch' may therefore be an abbreviation of this. Whatever its origins, there is no doubt that 'punch' spread to other European languages from English and since this occurred as trade with India was developing, the Indian associations must have had some influence on its usage.

Putting new wine into old bottles

This proverb alludes to the warning given by Christ in St Matthew's gospel, 'Neither do men put new wine into old bottles: else the bottles break, and the wine runneth out, and the bottles perish: but they put new wine into new bottles, and both are preserved.' The bottles referred to were made from animal skins, which, if old, were liable to split as new wine fermented inside them; new skins, however, were still sufficiently flexible to expand. In its figurative sense the proverb means that new ideas and practices cannot be successfully imposed on people who are too set in their ways to cope with the pressure of adjusting to them.

Putting the miller's eye out

The meaning of 'putting the miller's eye out' is similar to that of 'drowning the miller', referred to earlier. Here criticism is focused on a pudding, or broth, that has been made so thin that even the keen eye of a miller would be hard put to spot any flour in it.

Quarrel with your bread and butter

Since 'bread and butter' is applied to the fundamentals of life, such as basic food and the means of making a living, 'quarrelling with your bread and butter' is a way of saying that you are acting against your own interests, specifically with regard to recklessly giving up your job, or doing anything else that will deprive you of your living.

Ragout

Highly seasoned stews made by combining chopped meat and vegetables have been known as 'ragouts' in English since the seventeenth century. 'Ragout', like many cookery expressions, is French in origin, coming from *ragoûter*, derived from the Latin *regustare* meaning 'to taste again'. Both the Latin and French words have the sense of 'restoring taste', which in the case of a 'ragout' probably refers to the spicy seasoning added to it.

Red herring

Understanding the origin of this familiar saying is complicated by the fact that only part of it is generally said today. Representing anything that is used to divert attention from the principal issue that is being investigated or considered, the complete version of the phrase is 'drawing a red herring across the path'. Like kippers, herrings are traditionally dried, smoked and salted and have a strong smell, and it was popularly believed that if a 'red herring' was drawn across the path of a fox during a hunt it would cover the animal's scent and divert pursuing hounds into following a false trail.

Rehash

'Hash', as described earlier, is a meal made from chopped-up leftovers, scraps of food that have already been served once and are now being recycled. In the case of 'rehash', however, the allusion is more favourable than other, derogatory, connotations of the expressions associated with 'hash' such as 'making a hash of'. To 'rehash' something is to reconsider it, to cut it up, metaphorically, even finer than before and examine all the ins and outs before reaching a final conclusion.

Riddle of claret

A 'riddle of claret' is a specific quantity: thirteen bottles, comprising a magnum and twelve quarts. This was the amount customarily presented to some golf clubs by magistrates invited to celebration dinners. In accordance with tradition, the gift of claret was sent in a 'riddle', or coarse-meshed sieve.

Rod in pickle

Having 'a rod in pickle' means to 'have an unpleasant surprise in store for someone'. The allusion is to corporal punishment, which was once a regular feature of education and indeed chastisement in general. Birch rods used to administer such a beating were kept in brine (pickle) to ensure that the twigs remained supple.

Rotten apple

For as long as apples have been harvested and stored, wise apple-growers have avoided letting the fruits touch each other in the knowledge that a rotten apple will spread its disease by contagion. There are many proverbs based on this, including 'the rotten apple spoils its companion' and 'a rotten apple quickly infects its neighbour', which is the translation of an old Latin proverb 'the rotten apple injures its neighbour'. In its figurative sense, a 'rotten apple' refers to someone whose presence and influence has a demoralizing or otherwise deleterious effect on others, especially those in close proximity.

Row of beans

As one of the most readily available vegetables, the bean has frequently been regarded with low esteem. This phrase is usually used in a negative context such as, 'he isn't worth a row of beans', or 'I wouldn't give a row of beans for that', which values the bean as being of very little worth, even when it is sown in the traditional way to produce part of a crop.

Rub salt in the wound

It is common knowledge that salt added to an open wound will makes it sting and hurt even more. To deliberately 'rub salt in the wound' is therefore an action calculated to increase pain and discomfort. In its figurative use the phrase is applied to making an already painful subject worse. The same sense may be applied to 'rubbing something in', whereby an unpleasant situation is emphasized in order to prove a point, set an example or exact revenge.

Salad days

William Shakespeare is credited with coining this phrase in the lines spoken by Cleopatra right at the end of Act One of *Antony and Cleopatra* (1606), 'My salad days, / When I was green in judgement, cold in blood'. The 'salad days' the Queen of Egypt was referring to here were during an earlier period of her life when she had an affair with Julius Caesar, before she and Mark Antony fell in love. From Shakespeare, the phrase has become widely used to describe days of inexperience, when people are still 'green'. In 1954, British musical theatre writer Julian Slade borrowed the term as the title for his hugely popular musical *Salad Days*.

Salt and pepper

The contrasting colours of salt (white) and pepper (black) have led to their application to circumstances far removed from the kitchen and dinner table. Arguably one of the most common is the description of a dark-haired person beginning to turn grey, who is frequently described as having 'salt and pepper' on top.

SALT
AWAY

BEFORE REFRIGERATION WAS WIDELY AVAILABLE, PRESERVING FOOD IN BRINE OR BARRELS OF SALT WAS A COMMON METHOD OF SETTING ASIDE PROVISIONS FOR FUTURE CONSUMPTION. WHETHER AS A SUPPLY OF FOOD DURING THE UNPRODUCTIVE MONTHS OF WINTER, OR ON A SEA VOYAGE WHEN FRESH FOOD WAS UNAVAILABLE, SALTED FOOD COULD BE A LIFESAVER ON OCCASIONS. THE VALUE ATTACHED TO IT GAVE RISE TO THE EXPRESSION TO 'SALT AWAY', WHICH HAS THE SENSE OF 'STORING' OR 'PRESERVING FOR FUTURE USE'; IT IS APPLIED IN PARTICULAR TO MONEY THAT IS 'SALTED AWAY' AS A SAFEGUARD AGAINST LEAN TIMES IN THE FUTURE.

Salt of the earth

Salt was a vital commodity in the ancient world, so to be 'salt of the earth' was considered the ultimate endorsement, as seen in the biblical reference used by Christ to describe his disciples in the Sermon on the Mount: 'Rejoice, and be exceeding glad: for great is your reward in heaven: for so persecuted they the prophets which were before you. Ye are the salt of the earth.' From this point on, anyone described as the 'salt of the earth' could reasonably regard themselves as among the best of mankind.

Salt on his tail

This age-old piece of advice was often given to children who wanted to catch a bird. It was thought that sprinkling a bird's tail with salt would make it easier to catch, although this suggestion seems unlikely, not least because you would have to be very close to the bird anyway in order to do so. Nevertheless, the saying was transferred to people with the meaning of 'catching' or 'apprehending' someone.

Sandwich

The idea of placing food between two slices of bread may not have been dreamed up by the eighteenth-century aristocrat John Montagu, 4th Earl of Sandwich, but it was he who popularized it and gave the 'sandwich' its name. His lordship was an inveterate gambler, who would sit at the gaming table for hours on end (once for twenty-four hours non-stop). Such was his passion for cards that he begrudged having to leave the table even for meals and so got into the habit of calling for slices of meat between two pieces of bread to eat without the need to stop playing. For a time the Earl of Sandwich served as First Lord of the Admiralty and Captain Cook named the Sandwich Islands, in what is now Hawaii, after him.

Sandwich man

Since the middle of the nineteenth century, the men who carry advertising boards, front and back, as they walk about the streets have been known as 'sandwich men'. The allusion to the 'sandwich' comes from the method of carrying the boards – themselves known as sandwich boards – which are supported on straps slung over the carrier's shoulders, giving him the appearance of being 'sandwiched' between the two.

Sardine

The island of Sardinia and the small member of the herring family called the 'sardine' in English are closely related in their Greek and Latin names; one no doubt giving its name to the other, though which came first is uncertain. Sardines are caught all over the Mediterranean, not just in the waters around Sardinia.

Sauce

The word 'sauce' has been used in English since the fourteenth century to describe different flavoured liquid preparations that are added to many types of food to add moistness and taste. The English usage is a direct borrowing from French, which in turn came from the Latin *salsus*. However, *salsus* simply means 'flavoured with salt' and it took hundreds of years for the term to be applied to the wide range of flavoured sauces prepared by cooks today – in Roman times 'sauces' were effectively side dishes of vegetables seasoned with salt, which accompanied the main course. No doubt the idea of adding seasoning to enhance the flavour of food lay at the root of the usage of 'sauce' to mean 'insolence' and 'impertinence', as in phrases such as 'saucy devil!' and the ironic 'I like your sauce!'.

Saving your bacon

There are two theories as to why this expression conveys the idea of saving oneself from injury or harm. The first is based on the importance of 'bacon' as the principal meat that was salted and preserved for the lean winter months. Undoubtedly, the diligent housewife would take steps to prevent such a store from being tampered with, or raided, to ensure her family was catered for until spring. However, the second explanation is based on the idea that the Anglo-Saxon word for 'back' was *baec*, which was also the Old Dutch word for 'bacon'. Therefore to 'save your bacon' was quite literally to save your back from a thrashing.

Say 'cheese'

Since the 1920s it has been common for photographers to get their subjects to smile by asking them to say 'cheese'. A look in the mirror will confirm that saying 'cheese' does indeed put the lips in a position similar to a smile.

Saying grace

'Grace' said before a meal asks for blessing on food about to be eaten, while 'grace' said after a meal gives thanks for that food. Until the fourteenth century the phrase was commonly used in the plural, 'graces', following the French for 'thanks', *grâces*. In its earliest English usage it formed part of the old phrase to 'do graces' or to 'give graces', which again followed the French phrase of the same meaning, *rendre grâces*.

Selling like hot cakes

In America, 'pancakes' have been called 'hot cakes' for over 300 years. As a popular feature of the American diet, 'hot cakes' are cooked and sold at many social gatherings and such is the demand for them that they often sell as soon as they are cooked. Anything that 'sells likes hot cakes' is therefore a commercial triumph.

Serving the same sauce

This expression means to 'give as good as you get' and to 'retaliate' in kind. Here sauce is seen as a common denominator, in this instance in an argument or conflict, much as it is in the expression 'what's sauce for the goose is sauce for the gander'.

Settling on the lees

Lees occur in wine making in the form of sediment that collects at the bottom of a bottle or barrel. As such, they are the dregs that are thrown away after the wine has been removed. Anyone obliged to 'settle on the lees' is forced to resort to settling down on what remains after the best has gone, in other words making do with what is left after the main part of one's resources have been consumed, often recklessly.

Shoeing the goose

The idea of 'shoeing a goose' in the same way that one 'shoes' a horse is, of course, farcical. And that is the purpose of this expression. In its use of hyperbole, it points up the absurdity of the idea and by association implies how time can be wasted on unnecessary work and, worse still, how it can be frittered away by spending time on trifles rather than concentrating on things that really need to be done.

Short commons

At one time students at the universities of Oxford and Cambridge were served all their meals at common tables in their college halls. 'Commons' was the name given to the food served at breakfast and anyone receiving 'short commons' got 'short rations', in other words they were given only a scanty meal.

SIRLOIN

THERE HAVE BEEN VARIOUS STORIES TOLD OF AT LEAST THREE ENGLISH KINGS WHO WERE SAID TO HAVE 'KNIGHTED' THIS PARTICULAR JOINT OF BEEF, THEREBY ACCOUNTING FOR THE 'SIR' IN 'SIRLOIN'. HOWEVER, THE HISTORY OF THE WORD SHOWS THAT WHAT IS NOW SPELT 'SIRLOIN' SHOULD REALLY BE SPELT 'SURLOIN'. THIS IS BECAUSE THE WORD ORIGINATED IN OLD FRENCH AS *SURLOIGNE*, MEANING 'ABOVE THE LOIN', WITH REFERENCE TO THE JOINT'S POSITION ON THE ANIMAL. TO ADD TO THE CONFUSION, A 'BARON' OF BEEF, WHICH IS TWO UNSEPARATED 'SIRLOINS', ACQUIRED ITS NAME THROUGH THE INACCURATE SPELLING OF 'SUR/SIR', THE ASSUMPTION BEING THAT A 'BARON' WAS RANKED HIGHER THAN A KNIGHT.

Slippery as an eel

Eels crop up in several expressions and all draw on the difficulty of grasping an eel and preventing it from slipping away. 'Holding the eel of science by the tail' means to have a smattering of a subject, which is likely to slip from the memory as easily as an eel would slip from your grasp if held by the tail. Therefore anyone described as being as 'slippery as an eel' is regarded as being very evasive and, in certain cases, dishonest.

Small beer

'Small beer' was beer brewed with a low level of alcohol, thus 'small' in this expression means 'weak'. Unlike stronger, more alcoholic beers, 'small beer' did not 'pack a punch', nor did it need to be 'treated with respect' to avoid becoming intoxicated. By analogy, 'trivialities' and people regarded as being of 'little consequence' were dismissed as being 'small beer'.

Smart cookie

In Scotland a 'cookie' is a 'bun', whereas in America it is a small cake, probably from the Dutch *koekje*, which is the diminutive of *koek* ('cake'). In America 'cookie' became a term of endearment during the twentieth century and the term 'smart cookie' was bestowed on those blessed with shrewdness and quick wits.

Sour grapes

The disparaging tone of the phrase 'sour grapes' touches on a deeply rooted failing in human nature. This was taken up by Aesop in his fable about the fox who spotted a bunch of grapes and tried in vain to eat them – only when he realized that they were beyond his reach did he lose his initial enthusiasm. Turning away from the grapes, the fox dismissed the idea of eating them claiming that they were sour anyway. The story and its theme gained currency and, in time, something disparaged because it is beyond one's reach was referred to as 'sour grapes'.

Spare at the spigot and spill at the bung

A 'spigot' is a small peg or plug, which is inserted into the vent hole of a barrel or cask and here the allusion is to one filled with beer or wine. As a metaphor, this saying points to the owner's meanness over small things. By taking excessive care not to waste any of the barrel's valuable contents at the vent hole he overlooks the main bung sealing the barrel, through which his drink is leaking in profusion. To 'spare at the spigot and spill at the bung' therefore means to be tight-fisted about things that don't really matter, while being wasteful when it comes to those which really are important.

Spilling the beans

'Spilling the beans' is the inadvertent divulging of information that would otherwise have been kept secret. The origin of the phrase has been linked to a voting system in ancient Greece, where it was customary for beans of two different colours to be used in secret ballots, held among members of an organization to which a would-be member was applying. Those in favour of his joining voted with a white bean, signifying 'yes', while those against used a brown bean, which counted as a 'no' vote. When all votes had been cast, the beans were counted in secret, so that the prospective member would have no idea how many votes there were for and against him – the only way to discover this was if the beans were accidentally spilt in his presence. Another line of thought follows the idea that some fortune-tellers used beans instead of crystal balls or tea leaves, spilling the beans from a cup to create a pattern from which the future could supposedly be interpreted.

Spoon-fed

From the turn of the twentieth century, 'spoon-fed' has been used to describe two types of people who are prevented from acting independently, the first being those who are so cosseted and pampered that they are treated like babies. The second group to which this saying refers is the type of person who suffers a form of brainwashing and is 'spoon fed' ideas and information, which they consume without thinking for themselves.

Spring chicken

This American expression is usually used in a negative context – when a woman is described as being 'no spring chicken' the insinuation is that she is no longer in her prime. 'Chicken' and 'chick' have been slang expressions for girls and young women since the eighteenth century. The term 'spring chicken', however, came into use at the beginning of the twentieth century, although its use in reference to women is nonsensical because in the poultry business 'spring chickens' are actually young cockerels sent to market in the autumn.

Square meal

There is no definite evidence to explain where this phrase originates. However, it has been suggested that it comes from the predecessors of an essential item of crockery. Long before plates as we know them were in common use, food was served on 'trenchers', which were made from square-cut slices of stale brown bread hollowed out in the centre. A wealthy man would have several trenchers for his use during a meal, the more humble just one or two. At the end of the meal, the trenchers would be gathered up and given to the poor. In time, wood took over from bread and the new-look trencher was thus a wooden square, again with a large hole in the centre but with the addition of a small hollow in one corner for salt. If plentiful, the food would be piled in the centre of the square, thus providing a full and satisfying 'square meal'.

Staff of life

Since biblical times, bread has been regarded as one of mankind's basic foods, something simple and nourishing, which can be relied upon when other, more exotic, food is wanting. As such, bread has long been regarded as an important, if not vital, part of man's survival and from early Egyptian times was described as being 'the staff of life', the prop and support on which human existence could depend.

Stew in your own juice

Those who 'stew in their own juice' suffer the consequences of their actions and, by implication, suffer them for a considerable length of time. 'Stewing', both in the culinary and metaphorical sense, involves a slow, simmering process. Inside an enclosed cooking vessel, a mixture of meat and vegetables is gently stewed to produce a succulent, tasty meal in which the liquor the food has been cooking in is as important a factor in its taste as the solid ingredients. The meaning of the phrase is that those who adopt a particular course of action and metaphorically put their 'ingredients' into the melting pot must expect the consequences of their actions.

Storm in a teacup

Here is another use of hyperbole to point up the absurdity of a situation. At the risk of stating the obvious, a genteel cup of tea is not the place in which to find a 'storm'. However, the very circumstances in which tea is drunk from teacups imply that even slight deviations from the accepted code of conduct and conversation can cause ructions completely out of proportion to the real nature of any 'offence'. A 'storm in a teacup', therefore, is a 'great fuss made about something of no consequence'. In America the expression is more commonly found as 'a tempest in a teapot'.

SUNDAE

IN AMERICA, THERE WAS, AT ONE TIME, A LAW IN THE STATE OF VIRGINIA PROHIBITING THE SALE OF SODA-FOUNTAIN DRINKS ON SUNDAYS. HOWEVER, BECAUSE THERE CONTINUED TO BE A DEMAND FOR SUCH DRINKS ON SUNDAYS AN ENTERPRISING DRUGSTORE OWNER DECIDED TO CREATE A 'THICKENED' DRINK BY ADDING FRUIT AND ICE CREAM TO HIS SODA FOUNTAIN DRINKS. ONCE THE CONSISTENCY OF THE DRINK REACHED A LEGALLY DEFINED LEVEL, IT BECAME CLASSIFIED AS A MEAL AS FAR AS THE LAW WAS CONCERNED AND WAS NO THEREFORE NO LONGER RESTRICTED TO MONDAY TO SATURDAY SALES. FROM THE POINT OF VIEW OF THE DRUGSTORE CUSTOMERS, IT WAS A 'SUNDAY' DRINK AND BEFORE LONG HAD ACQUIRED THE NAME 'SUNDAE'.

Taking eggs for money

There was a time when eggs were so readily available that they were sold for next to nothing. This gave rise to the expression 'to take eggs for money', meaning that you 'allow yourself to be imposed upon'. The allusion here is that you are prepared to receive payment for something that would normally be made available for significantly less than is being offered.

Taking the biscuit

To 'take the biscuit' can be interpreted in two ways, depending on whether it is being used ironically or not. As a straightforward statement of approbation, 'taking the biscuit' means being 'the best of the lot', even being 'incredible'. However, it is commonly used to express a strong degree of irony, for example 'I've heard some daft things in my time, but that takes the biscuit!' 'Taking the biscuit' is an Anglicized form of an expression common in America from the middle of the nineteenth century, which referred to 'taking the cake', an allusion to the cake awarded to the winners of a 'cakewalk', a popular pastime, particularly amongst Black Americans, in which couples walked arm in arm around a room. The couple judged to be the most graceful walkers 'took the cake' as their prize.

Taking the say

'Taking the say' is an abbreviated form of 'taking the assay'. In modern usage, an 'assay' is a test applied to metal alloys, but in the sixteenth century the term referred to 'tests' in general – in the case of 'taking the say', the 'test' was one on food and drink. In an age when assassination by poisoning was not unheard of, food and drink prepared for anyone at risk of being murdered was 'tested' and 'tasted' before it was laid before them in order to prove that it was safe to be consumed.

Talking turkey

This expression, meaning 'talking business' or 'talking seriously', originated in America where it was in common usage by the middle of the nineteenth century before spreading throughout the English-speaking world. It appears to date from the early days of the colonies, when turkeys formed an important part of the trade between the Native Americans and the Pilgrim Fathers. Before long, the Native Americans realized that every trading visit was likely to involve their supplying turkeys and thus 'You come to talk turkey?' became a familiar saying whenever a colonist appeared to discuss business.

Tea and sympathy

This well-known expression has come to refer to a sympathetic listener who offers comfort to someone in distress. The term was known by the twentieth century, but gained a boost when it was used as the title for a 1956 film starring Deborah Kerr, which was based on a stage play of 1953 of the same name by Robert Anderson and told the story of a schoolboy's affair with a teacher's wife.

Teetotal

Since the middle of the nineteenth century, the term 'teetotal' has been used to describe anyone who abstains from all types of alcoholic drink. 'Teetotal' came into use on both sides of the Atlantic at more or less the same time, though each has a distinct origin of its own. In England the word appears to have been coined by Dick Turner of Preston in Lancashire. Speaking at a temperance meeting in September 1833, he declared the need for complete abstinence and emphasized the point by telling his audience that 'nothing but the tee-total would do'. Such was the success of his speech, that 'teetotal' was quickly adopted as the name for total abstinence and his tombstone bears the inscription 'Beneath this stone are deposited the remains of Richard Turner, author of the word *Teetotal* as applied to abstinence from all intoxicating liquors …'. In America, however, the phrase may have appeared slightly earlier as a result of campaigning by the New York Temperance Society. Members who signed the 'pledge' had 'O.P.' (standing for Old Pledge) entered against their names if they undertook to abstain from distilled spirits only. Those who pledged to abstain from all forms of alcohol had a 'T' for 'total abstinence' entered against their names. The regular use of 'T-total' soon led to the spelling 'teetotal'.

That's the way the cookie crumbles

The American 'cookie' probably takes its name from the Dutch *koekje*, meaning a 'little cake'; in Britain 'cookie' equates with 'biscuit'. The expression 'that's the way the cookie crumbles' gained in popularity after the Second World War as a fatalistic expression meaning 'what will be, will be', usually when something turns out less promisingly than expected. Popularized by American advertisements of the 1950s, the phrase is now widely used in the English-speaking world as a whole.

The answer is a lemon

This is a form of response meaning 'nothing doing', which is given in reply to a request or question regarded as being unreasonable or ridiculous. The tart taste of lemon juice has caused the fruit to be associated with the negative side of many issues and in this case 'the answer is a lemon' amounts to saying 'you must be joking!'.

The fat is in the fire

Anyone who has cooked over an open fire knows the hazards of letting grease or fat fall into the flames. Since most cooking took place over open fires until as recently as the nineteenth century, fat falling into the fire was a constant problem and worry. Occurring in various forms in several languages, 'the fat is in the fire' has been used in English since the Middle Ages in the sense of something having been let out accidentally, which results in a 'flare-up'.

The mill cannot grind with the water that is past

First recorded in the early years of the seventeenth century, this age-old proverb dates from a time when watermills ground much of the flour in Britain and implies that opportunities should be taken when they are presented, because once they have moved past they cannot be retrieved.

The moon is made of green cheese

Anyone who believes that 'the moon is made of green cheese' must be a simpleton – at least that is the gist of this long-established expression. Known in English for around 500 years, 'the moon is made of green cheese' means the same today as it did in King Henry VIII's reign – that anyone who believes anything as absurd as that would believe absolutely anything.

There's no such thing as a free lunch

The idea that you can't get something for nothing had been in circulation long before this expression was coined in America during the nineteenth century and enthusiastically adopted by economists in the second half of the twentieth century. It appears to have developed from the practice of some saloons, which offered 'free' food to those who patronized them in order to drink. Presumably the prices of drinks were raised accordingly, because many saloons exhibited signs warning 'no free lunch here' to anyone hoping to eat without buying a drink. The practice had died out before the First World War, partly because of changes to licensing and health legislation that tightened up on the insanitary conditions in which 'free lunches' were served in the less salubrious establishments.

The world's mine oyster

In the Middle Ages, oysters were recognized as both a source of nourishment and as the producers of precious pearls. The phrase 'the world's mine oyster' was used in the sense of 'the world is the place from which a profit can be extracted' by William Shakespeare when he gave Pistol the line 'Why, then the world's mine oyster, / Which I with sword will open' after Falstaff has refused to lend him a penny in the second act of *The Merry Wives of Windsor*, published in 1602.

Thinking small potatoes

Although the potato arrived in English-speaking countries fewer than 500 years ago, it soon became well embedded in several common expressions, of which 'thinking small potatoes' is one of the oldest – in British usage the saying originally referred to 'little potatoes', but 'small' became the standard wording in America and was later adopted elsewhere . 'Small potatoes' means 'something of little consequence', and to 'think small potatoes' is therefore to regard something as being of very little importance.

Titbit

First coined as 'tydbit' or 'tidbit', the word 'titbit' has been used to describe a tasty morsel since the seventeenth century. A combination of 'tid', meaning 'nice' and 'soft', and 'bit', derived from 'bite', the expression carried the sense of something that had been 'bitten off'.

To cry cockles

This grim expression came into being when executions were still held in public. From the late eighteenth century to the middle of the nineteenth, 'to cry cockles' was slang for 'to be hanged'. The association comes from the gurgling sound of strangulation.

Toffee-nosed

Describing someone as 'toffee-nosed' implies that they are 'stuck-up', giving themselves pretensions with the aim of appearing superior. While it is tempting to link the stickiness of 'toffee' with the allusion to being 'stuck up', the latter refers to the male peacock, whose magnificent tail plumage is 'stuck up' as a sign of his superiority over others. 'Toffee-nosed' may owe more to the nineteenth-century slang 'toff'. This was a term applied to noblemen and gentlemen commoners: students of aristocratic backgrounds at the University of Oxford who were allowed to wear caps ('mortar boards') with gold tassels, or tufts. 'Toff' is a corruption of 'tuft', so someone who sets themselves up as a 'toff' and adopts a haughty demeanour could well be described as 'toffee-nosed'.

To go the whole hog

To go 'the whole hog' means to do something completely and thoroughly, with no half measures. The expression may have derived from the practice of using every part of the household pig, leaving nothing to waste after the animal had been butchered so that meat could be set aside to last over the winter. Another explanation rests on a different meaning of 'hog', which, from the end of the seventeenth century, was slang for a 'shilling'. In this context 'to go the whole hog' means 'to spend the whole shilling at once.' In both cases the phrase has an air of determination and resolution that survives today.

To have a bone to pick

'To have a bone to pick' implies that a person has something disagreeable to discuss and settle with someone. The allusion is to a bone thrown to dogs, which inevitably leads to snarling and fighting as each tries to win the bone for its own enjoyment.

To have your cake and eat it

Recorded in English writer and playwright John Heywood's *Dialogue of Proverbs* of 1546 as 'I trowe ye raue, Wolde ye bothe eate your cake, and have your cake?', the wording in this well-known saying may have changed since then – 'eat' and 'have' are interchangeable in all versions – but the meaning has remained the same: 'you cannot have it both ways'. Once the 'cake' has been 'eaten', it cannot be retained in your possession – when the reference is to money, the implication is that money spent cannot be spent a second time, nor can it be saved.

To make mincemeat

An abbreviation of 'minced meat', i.e. meat that has been cut into very small pieces, the word 'mincemeat' derives from the Latin *minutia*, meaning 'smallness' and 'fineness', via the Old French *mincier*. Used figuratively, to 'make mincemeat' of someone is to 'demolish' and 'defeat' them completely.

Too many cooks spoil the broth

As one of the best known 'food' proverbs, 'too many cooks spoil the broth' has been recorded in English since Shakespeare's time. Its meaning, which has remained unaltered, is that if too many people take part in an undertaking its chances of success will be prejudiced.

Tough cookie

In the expression 'smart cookie', 'cookie' is an endearment used in much the same way as 'sweetheart'. However, such an endearment would be inappropriate in the case of 'tough cookie', which describes an intractable person, best summed up as an 'awkward customer'.

Tripe

'Tripe' was once a more popular dish than it is today. Formed from the first or second stomach of an ox, tripe was eaten in ancient times and was widely enjoyed throughout Europe. By the nineteenth century, however, 'tripe' or a 'bag of tripe' was a term of a disparagement in English slang. By the beginning of the twentieth century 'tripe' was starting to be seen as an inferior type of food and so became associated with 'rubbish' and 'complete nonsense'. This applied particularly when 'tripe' referred to writing, acting or singing of a very inferior standard and this is the sense in which it is used today.

True blue will never stain

A 'true blue' is a person who is constant, loyal, faithful and reliable. Such a person is reckoned never to disgrace himself and the allusion in 'true blue will never stain' is to the blue aprons traditionally worn by butchers, which do not show blood stains.

TRUE TO YOUR SALT

'SALT' IN THIS CONTEXT MEANS 'SALARY', WHICH COMES FROM THE LATIN *SALARIUS* MEANING 'TO DO WITH SALT' AND REFERS TO THE ALLOWANCE PAID TO ROMAN SOLDIERS TO BUY SALT. THEREFORE, ANYONE SAID TO BE 'TRUE TO HIS SALT', WAS 'TRUE TO HIS SALARY' AND BY ASSOCIATION 'TRUE TO HIS EMPLOYERS'.

Up corn, down horn

This old saying refers to variations of commodity prices in the agricultural market. 'Corn' applies to cereal crops; 'horn' to beef. 'Up corn, down horn' means that when the price of corn is high (making it expensive), the price of beef is low (making it cheap) because people have less money to spend on meat.

Upper crust

One explanation for the origin of this phrase lies in what was believed to be a long-established practice of offering the upper crust, regarded as the tastiest part, of a loaf of bread to the most honoured guest seated at table, thus giving them the best share. Another suggestion is that the 'upper crust' referred to is in fact a pie crust, which was also reckoned to be the best part of a pie. In both explanations 'upper crust' has a sense of superiority and this is the meaning to which it is put figuratively in referring to an elite or highest social class.

Venison

'Venison' has a very specific meaning today as the flesh of a deer, but this is comparatively recent. When 'venison' was first recorded in English in the thirteenth century, it referred to the flesh of any animal killed in a hunt. The original meaning and the word itself derived from the Latin *venatio*, the noun for 'hunting' or 'the chase'.

Vintage

'Vintage' is the English form of the French *vendange*, the 'wine harvest' that takes place each autumn when the grapes are picked, and is therefore the word used to classify wines by year. Wines of a good 'vintage' are those made when the growing conditions have resulted in a harvest of grapes of very high quality. Thus wine from a good *vendange* is known in English as 'vintage wine', and from this 'vintage year' has been applied to memorable or noteworthy years in any context. 'Vintage' and *vendange* originated from the Latin for 'a grape-gathering', *vindemenia*.

Vol-au-vent

The literal translation from French for this popular pastry dish filled with creamed meat or chicken is 'flight on the wind'. This probably alludes to the very light puff-pastry from which the case of a vol-au-vent is made.

Waffle

Both 'waffle' and the Dutch *wafel*, from which it was originally coined in America, are used to describe a batter cake baked in a grid-like pattern between two irons of that shape. Since the end of the nineteenth century, 'waffle' has acquired the pejorative meaning of 'nonsense' and 'meaningless chatter'. This may be due to its similarity to a number of other words. Two of the strongest contenders are the Scottish 'waffle', meaning to 'flutter' or 'flap', and the dialect use of 'waffle' for the yelping sound made by a small dog.

Walking on eggshells

The analogy of walking on 'eggshells' (sometimes 'eggs') has been used since the seventeenth century to describe the act of treading very lightly but in the metaphorical sense of trying not to cause any disturbance.

Waygoose

It was traditional to serve goose at the annual entertainment given to printers, originally held at Bartholomew tide on the 24 August and marking the change of seasons from summer to autumn, when it became necessary to start working by candlelight. The term was later applied to an annual feast held earlier in the summer. The origin of 'waygoose' or 'wayzgoose' appears to be from 'wayz', an obsolete word for 'stubble', which may have referred to a goose being allowed to feed on the corn dropped amongst the stubble during harvest, which would have started a few weeks before Bartholomew tide.

WELSH RAREBIT

A DISH OF MELTED CHEESE AND SEASONING, POURED OVER HOT BUTTERED TOAST, 'WELSH RAREBIT' WAS FIRST COINED AS 'WELSH RABBIT' AND WAS KNOWN BY THIS NAME UNTIL THE END OF THE EIGHTEENTH CENTURY. THE REASON THAT 'RABBIT' WAS CHANGED TO 'RAREBIT' APPEARS TO HAVE BEEN LEXICAL INTERFERENCE BY A DICTIONARY COMPILER. UNABLE TO FIND ANY CONNECTION BETWEEN THE DISH AND A RABBIT, HE SEEMS TO HAVE DECIDED TO CHANGE THE NAME TO SOMETHING MORE APPROPRIATE. THE NAME 'WELSH RAREBIT' HAS STUCK, BUT HAD 'WELSH RABBIT' BEEN ALLOWED TO SURVIVE IT WOULD HAVE SAT HAPPILY IN THE DICTIONARY ALONGSIDE OTHER CULINARY ANOMALIES SUCH AS 'BOMBAY DUCK', WHICH IS REALLY A FISH, AND 'MOCK TURTLE SOUP', WHICH IS ACTUALLY MADE FROM A CALF'S HEAD.

Wetting your whistle

'Wetting your whistle' is an idiom that was in common use when Chaucer was writing the *Canterbury Tales* at the end of the fourteenth century; he uses it in *The Reeve's Tale*, in the line 'So was hir joly whistle wel ywet'. The meaning is the same now as it was then: 'wetting your whistle' equates to 'having a drink'.

What's sauce for the goose is sauce for the gander

This proverb, dating from the seventeenth century, means 'what is suitable for a woman is suitable for a man'. An earlier version makes the same assertion with cattle, but this has not stood the test of time. The wording of the proverb appears in different forms as well, but the meaning has remained the same throughout its history.

Where's the beef?

'Where's the beef?' became a catchphrase in the 1984 US presidential election campaign. Walter Mondale, who was canvassing for, and eventually won, the Democratic Party nomination, used 'Where's the beef?' to great effect in pointing up the inadequacies of his rivals' arguments and promises. The phrase had actually been coined as part of a nationwide advertising campaign by the Wendy's hamburger chain. This included a television commercial featuring three elderly ladies who ordered hamburgers in a restaurant styled 'home of the Big Bun'. While there was no disputing the size of the bun, the tiny sliver of meat inside was not to their liking and one of the trio was moved to telephone the restaurant manager to demand angrily, 'Where's the beef?' From this, the phrase acquired its broader meaning of questioning the substance of a statement or promise made by someone else.

Whisky

'Whisky' is the modern name for the famous spirit distilled (with this spelling) in Scotland from malted barley; in Ireland and America the spirit is known as 'whiskey'. It comes from the Gaelic *uisge beatha*, meaning 'the water of life' in the same sense as *aqua vita* in Latin and *eau de vie* in French.

With a pinch of salt

Anything taken 'with a pinch of salt' is treated with the utmost suspicion. Just as a 'pinch of salt' may help you swallow otherwise unpalatable food, so a metaphoric 'pinch of salt' enables you to accept something dubious by granting it a mere grain of truth.

Without a bean

Once an important part of the poor man's diet, beans are so common that they have long been regarded as having little financial value. The story of Jack and the Beanstalk confirms this: Jack's mother is furious when he comes home having 'sold' their cow for a few beans. So to be 'without a bean' is to be very hard up, as in the expression 'I haven't a bean' which means 'I haven't any money at all'.

Working for peanuts

'Peanuts' are not really nuts at all – strictly speaking they are legumes and belong to the same family as peas. In fact 'peanuts' are about the same size as peas, which makes them smaller than most other nuts and it is their size that has led to their being associated with 'meagreness'. This applies particularly when peanuts are used metaphorically for money and therefore anyone 'working for peanuts' is working for something very small, in other words for 'very low wages'.

You can't make an omelette without breaking eggs

This apposite saying is a direct translation of a French proverb and carries a clear warning – anyone who hopes to 'get something for nothing' is unlikely to succeed unless they are prepared to make the necessary effort or sacrifice to achieve their objective.

You can't make a soufflé rise twice

A 'soufflé' is a light and fluffy baked or steamed egg dish, made by mixing a thick sauce or purée with the yolks and stiffly beaten whites of eggs. The secret of its success is serving it directly from the oven, before it begins to sag and lose its consistency. The one thing the great majority of cooks are unable to do is to 'make a soufflé rise twice'. The expression gained wider currency in the twentieth century in the sense of 'it is pointless trying make something happen a second time if it is unrepeatable'. The wider implication of the expression is that a unique event should be allowed to remain unique, since trying to recreate it will only debase the memory of the original.